Contents

4

1. Easy-Believism.

Before writing this, I was arduously surfing the web for a book that defends Easy-Believism but to no avail. In fact, most of the literature I found was outright against it. I did however find a few short writings that espoused a correct understanding of Easy-Believism.

My understanding of this doctrine doesn't undermine scripture at all. Easy-Believism is simply believing that Christ died for all your sins and loving Him because of it. Putting complete trust in Him as your Savior. It is no different than Sola Fide, so I opted to write about this newfangled doctrine in this book.

After many minutes of discouragement resulting in no such online book on Easy-Believism, I discovered that I already had a book that was far more superior to any other man-written book.

The Bible!

It backs up this doctrine profusely.

(During my Internet endeavors…)

As I browsed through the online Christian websites or so-called Christian websites, I saw many litigious subjects, lots of debates and too many dogmatic hardheads trying to prove their points. I, myself, am a dogmatic hardhead, but only a dogmatic hardhead for the <u>truth</u>! Some might ask me why do I think that I have an authority in addressing doctrinal truth. My only response would be because I have honestly consulted the Bible in order to document the truth. I have also — to the best of my ability and with God's help — made sure that my points are incontrovertible.

2 Peter 1:20.

Knowing this first, that no prophecy of the scripture is of any private interpretation.

I've come across so many websites that try to refute the neo-popular doctrine of Easy-Believism. What is Easy-Believism, you may be wondering? It is the idea that salvation comes from simple faith in Christ and nothing else.

Most of the anti-Easy-Believism websites were just junk-sites. One was entitled: *Easy-Believism, the fast track to hell.*

I'm going to elaborate on Easy-Believism based on what the Bible says, not with what fallible man subjectively asserts.

John 3:36.

He that <u>believeth</u> on the Son hath everlasting life: and he that believeth not the Son shall not see life; but the wrath of God abideth on him.

Sounds pretty simple.

Let's look at some more verses.

John 6:40.

And this is the will of him that sent me, that every one which seeth the Son, and <u>believeth</u> on him, may have everlasting life: and I will raise him up at the last day.

John 11:26.

And whosoever liveth and <u>believeth</u> in me shall never die. Believest thou this?

To deny Easy-Believism is to add something to one's belief. Confession, baptism, tithing, works, ritual, perseverance … etc, etc, etc. But scripture refutes this.

John 6:28-29.

Then said they unto him, What shall we do, that we might work the works of God? Jesus answered and said unto them, This is the work of God, that ye <u>believe</u> on him whom he hath sent.

Belief is all the work necessary.

This verse alone totally whitewashes any "faith-plus-works" doctrines!

Jesus is so emphatic that Easy-Believism is true that He exhorts us to believe in Him even for diverse reasons.

John 14:11.

Believe me that I am in the Father, and the Father in me: or else believe me for the very works' sake.

In other words, believe because of His miracles.

Jesus just wants us to believe! Period.

The Amplified Bible lends clarity to this verse.

(Believe Me that I am in the Father and the Father in Me; or else believe Me for the sake of the (very) works themselves. (If you cannot trust Me, at least let these works that I do in My Father's name convince you.)

Anyone who opposes Easy-Believism after such clear divine revelation, once again must twist and torque scriptures out of its context to support their heretical doctrine.

What happened when Jesus was hung on the cross?

The thief on the right-hand side simply believed, declared it by asking to be remembered and was thus saved.

Luke 22:42-43.

Then he said to Jesus, Lord, remember me when You come in Your kingly glory! And He answered him, Truly I tell you, today you shall be with Me in Paradise.

Some people will say, *yeah, yeah, but that only applied to him because he couldn't come down off of the cross.* Coming off of the cross would mean that he would have to do penance, change his lifestyle, get baptized and whatnot.

This is ridiculous!

Salvation is for everyone and it is the same for everyone in terms of attainment (Acts 15:11). If some people had to do more than what the thief on the cross did, then salvation would be mutable, discriminatory and ambiguous at best. Easy-Believism is undoubtedly biblical and irrefutable! The thief on the cross represents the common bedside believer. Nothing left to do but believe in Jesus.

The only alternative to Easy-Believism is works and the only point in works is to get rewards in heaven. Works prove (to man) that we are saved.

James 2:18.

Yea, a man may say, Thou hast faith, and I have works: shew me thy faith without thy works, and I will shew thee my faith by my works.

Or in other words, prove your faith by works.

After we are saved, by Easy-Believism — we should — out of appreciation accomplish good deeds and it is important that we are diligent because our works will assure us rewards in heaven.

Mark 9:41.
For whosoever shall give you a cup of water to drink in my name, because ye belong to Christ, verily I say unto you, he shall not lose his reward.

Easy-Believism is biblically true. Because grace is a free gift and believing in Christ is simply receiving that gift. Receiving a gift is quite easy. In fact, it is easier than easy.

Easy-Believism is incontestably TRUE!

Christ said that we are to come as children.

If a child is to come to Christ, it must be pretty EASY!

Matthew 19:14.
But Jesus said, Suffer little children, and forbid them not, to come unto me: for of such is the kingdom of heaven.

To complicate Easy-Believism (the gospel) is once again to add to it. In many cases it is to add a sequential action or requisite.

Ephesians 2:8.

For by grace are ye saved through faith; and that not of yourselves: it is the gift of God.

I can't find where any additional requirements for salvation are indicated in scripture. In fact, scripture says that salvation is a one-time event. Receiving eternal life is activated by a one-time moment of faith in Jesus. He only had to die <u>once</u>. When you get baptized to symbolize that you've been saved by faith, it only happens <u>once</u>. There is only <u>one</u> God. Denying Sola Fide, Easy-Believism, free grace and other such essential doctrines creates a duality or plurality complex. If I'm saved by one singular action: faith — then what else do I have to do? The answer is: nothing!

Anything we do after receiving salvation has to do with sanctification and earning rewards in heaven.

Ephesians 4:4-6.

There is <u>one</u> body, and <u>one</u> Spirit, even as ye are called in <u>one</u> hope of your calling; One Lord, <u>one</u> faith, <u>one</u> baptism, <u>One</u> God and Father of all, who is above all, and through all, and in you all.

John 5:24.
Verily, verily, I say unto you, He that heareth my word, and BELIEVETH on him that sent me, hath everlasting life, and shall not come into condemnation; but is passed from death unto life.

God bless.

2. Keeping The Law.

There's so much junk out there about the law in Christian circles, websites, churches with flawed doctrines and especially in the mindsets of the opponents of Sola Fide. (OSFs.) I've heard so many uninformed people talk about the law being still in effect today. Which it is for our benefit, not our salvation. I've heard people say that Jesus removed the ceremonial law but not the Mosaic Law. I've heard people say that the Ten Commandments were easy to obey whereupon they denied that they even had sins in such areas as covetousness and envy. But later, the truth embarrassingly surfaced.

What I'm trying to say is that most of what I've heard is a bunch of gobbledygook coming from the mouths of people that don't study the Word of God. Some of the harsher remarks are explained in the following.

The law!

They slap you in the face with: <u>The law!</u> You gotta follow the law to the letter in order to be saved. I've unfortunately frequented websites that opposed the doctrine of eternal security using such scriptures as:

Revelation 22:14.

Blessed are those who follow his commandments, that they may have the right to the tree of life, and may enter through the gates into the city.

In other words, you won't make it to heaven unless you totally obey the commandments to the bitter end of life—and that's exactly what it would be in such a case, bitter! This nonsense advocates the idea that if you don't follow the commandments or the law then you can't be saved.

But they fail to realize that—we as Christians—aren't even under the law.

Galatians 5:18.

But if ye be led of the Spirit, ye are not under the law.

This is referring to Christians. How do we know? Unsaved people are not lead by the spirit. EVER!

Romans 8:1.

There is therefore now no condemnation to them which are in Christ Jesus, who walk not after the flesh, but after the Spirit.

So, we, Christians, spirit-lead followers of Christ, are not even under the law.

To take this to a deeper level, I've posited what it means to keep the law according to the Bible. And before I expound, let me emphatically say that now law-keeping or lawbreaking has anything to do with salvation. (Galatians 2:16.)

Keeping The Law Is By Love!

Such verses instruct us to keep the law.

John 15:10.

If ye keep my commandments, ye shall abide in my love; even as I have kept my Father's commandments, and abide in his love.

Leviticus 22:31.

Therefore shall ye keep my commandments, and do them: I am the LORD.

Numbers 15:40.

That ye may remember, and do all my commandments, and be holy unto your God.

Deuteronomy 8:6.

Therefore thou shalt keep the commandments of the LORD thy God, to walk in his ways, and to fear him.

Psalm 119:35.

Make me to go in the path of thy commandments; for therein do I delight.

Ecclesiastes 12:13.

Let us hear the conclusion of the whole matter: Fear God, and keep his commandments: for this is the whole duty of man.

Clearly, these verses instruct us to keep the commandments. And we should, but it is not for the sake of salvation. We, as sinful Christians couldn't perfectly obey them all even on our best day. So, listen to what the solution to this problem is.

Matt 22:37-40.

37. Jesus replied: "'Love the Lord your God with all your heart and with all your soul and with all your mind.

38. This is the first and great commandment.

39. And the second is like unto it, Thou shalt love thy neighbour as thyself.

40. On these two commandments hang all the law and the prophets.

It is brotherly love towards God (the first commandment) and towards one another (the second commandment) that fulfills the entire law, not obedience or dutiful works.

Read on…

Galatians 5:14.

For all the law is fulfilled in one word, even in this; Thou shalt love thy neighbour as thyself.

James 2:8.

If ye fulfil the royal law according to the scripture, Thou shalt love thy neighbour as thyself, ye do well.

What this is saying is that if you love your neighbor, you have fulfilled the royal law and have done well in so doing.

Romans 13:8.

Owe no man any thing, but to love one another: for he that loveth another hath fulfilled the law.

Romans 13:10.

Love worketh no ill to his neighbour: therefore love is the fulfilling of the law.

So how do we fulfill the law? Simple. By loving God and our neighbors. God, through the Holy Spirit, enables us to love one another. It's not a way to earn salvation, which is through faith alone. Love, for one another and for God comes naturally when the Holy Spirit is immanent in us. Don't get me wrong; I'm not saying that you have to "like" everybody. I can understand the dislike for terrorists and the hatred for terrorism as a general principle. But "love" and "like" are two totally different concepts. So, don't think that I am adding unto grace, … the deed of love. True godly love is only possible for those that are in Christ.

Otherwise, it is love in vain, like paternal love, instinctual love, hormonal love, material love or animal love.

Keeping the Law Is By Faith or Belief.

Romans 10:4.

For Christ is the end of the law for righteousness to every one that <u>believeth.</u>

Galatians 2:16.

Knowing that a man is not justified by the works of the law, but by the <u>faith</u> of Jesus Christ, even we have <u>believed</u> in Jesus Christ, that we might be justified by the <u>faith</u> of Christ, and not by the works of the law: for by the works of the law shall no flesh be justified.

Galatians 3:11.

Clearly no one is justified before God by the law, because, "The righteous will live by faith."

Galatians 3:18.

For if the inheritance be of the law, it is no more of promise: but God gave it to Abraham by promise.

Romans 4:3.

For what saith the scripture? Abraham <u>believed</u> God, and it was counted unto him for righteousness.

(Also look at Genesis 15:6 for more on the Abrahamic covenant.)

Galatians 3:24.

Wherefore the law was our schoolmaster to bring us unto Christ, that we might be justified by <u>faith.</u>

These scriptures are overtly clear that salvation is by "faith" or "belief" alone! You can't add anything to them. But the opponents of (OSF's) must erroneously add to them in order to support their warped doctrine of works or conditional salvation. That's dishonest, unbiblical, heretical, manipulative and unchristian. Read what scripture says about such people.

2 Peter 3:16.

As also in all his epistles, speaking in them of these things; in which are some things hard to be understood, which they that are <u>unlearned</u> and <u>unstable</u> wrest, as they do also the other scriptures, unto their own destruction.

I myself don't know too many people that are wise and sound in doctrine, whom wrest and contort scriptures out of context. In fact, most of the OSFs or Works Salvationists, and or any other kind of heretic for that matter have proven to be very <u>unlearned</u> and <u>unstable</u>. And I've also noticed that they are deceitful and even arrogantly intolerant of such doctrines as Sola Fide. The point is this. Scripture twisting and manipulation is a telltale sign of unlearned, unstable ignorance and even prejudice.

We are saved by faith alone. Period!

****

As Christians we should know that we are saved. The importance of salvific assurance is very crucial for spiritual growth. I hope this book will engender much spiritual fructification. (Fruitfulness.)

Ephesians 3:19.

And to know the love of Christ, which passeth knowledge, that ye might be filled with all the fulness of God.

We couldn't know this if we had to literally obey the law in order to be saved. If that were the case, we'd have to keep daily journals and we'd spend way too much time trying (and failing) to behave like perfect little angels. When would we ever conclude that we were truly, finally saved? The answer is: Never! The only hope we have in knowing that we are truly saved, in the present tense, is to know that it is by faith alone.

The main point here is that Jesus obeyed the law for us.

Philippians 2:8.

And being found in fashion as a man, he humbled himself, and became obedient unto death, even the death of the cross.

God bless.

3.What Sin?

1 John 3:9.

Whosoever is born of God doth not commit sin; for his seed remaineth in him: and he cannot sin, because he is born of God.

Logically and honestly, we both know that Christians still sin after salvation, so what is this verse talking about? Read it again and look at the diacritically underlined words.

Whosoever is born of God doth not commit sin; for <u>his</u> seed remaineth in him: and <u>he</u> cannot sin, because <u>he</u> is born of God.

<u>He</u> refers to the Christian. Yes, this is in the active indicative tense. But it is referring to who is not sinning. Compare this to Romans 7:20.

I used the Amplified Bible for clarity.

Romans 7:20.

Now if I do what I do not desire to do, it is no longer I doing it, but the sin which dwells within me.

Read this verse again and look at the underlined words.

Now if <u>I</u> (the Christian) do what <u>I</u> (the Christian) do not desire to do, it is no longer <u>I</u> (the Christian) doing it, but the sin which dwells within me.

We are not considered sinners in God's eyes if we are in Christ, nor are we identified by our sinful behavior.

We are considered: "Saints."

Psalm 30:4.

Sing to the Lord, O you <u>saints</u> of His, and give thanks at the remembrance of His holy name.

We are considered: "Sons of God."

Genesis 6:2.

That the <u>sons of God</u> saw the daughters of men that they were fair; and they took them wives of all which they chose.

We are considered "brothers" (brethren).

Matthew 28:10.

Then said Jesus unto them, Be not afraid: go tell my <u>brethren</u> that they go into Galilee, and there shall they see me.

Jesus was referring to His followers as "brethren," not "sinners."

We are considered: "children."

Matthew 18:3.

And said, Verily I say unto you, Except ye be converted, and become as <u>little children</u>, ye shall not enter into the kingdom of heaven.

Now a skeptic or an anti-SolaFidist might say that I'm just making all this up in order to support my doctrine. You'd have to really question Romans 7:20 in order to ratify such a claim.

You'd also have to try and figure out who these so-called elite Christians are that literally NO LONGER SIN!

Some will say that this is talking about Christians not <u>practicing</u> sin, but that leaves too many loose ends and too much opportunity for splitting hairs over what sinful practice entails or means. To those who would say that Christians sin, but aren't living in or practicing sin, read John 8:34.

Jesus answered them, Verily, verily, I say unto you, Whosoever committeth sin is the servant (or slave) of sin.

(Emphasis mine.)

This verse is not saying that you were a slave to sin before you were saved and now you no longer are a slave. This is referring to Christians as well. When you sin, at that moment you are a servant to sin. Fortunately, this slavery doesn't have to be fulltime.

The best example I can give would be someone looking at pornography. He engages for twelve minutes. Logically speaking, he was a slave to sin for twelve minutes. Afterwards, he shamefully reads his Bible for two hours. During those two hours he was not a slave to sin!

Some would still argue that this is referring to

practicing sin and not just arbitrarily slipping up—off the cuff. But in light of God's demanded perfection, is there really any difference? I can't imagine Saint Peter denying someone who was a slave to smoking cigarettes and addicted to reading MAD magazines an entrance into heaven and then allowing some pious zealot into heaven all because he slipped up only a few times by calling his wife a foul word.

I would have to say that both are less than perfect. And God demands perfection!

Compare this scripture with 1 John 3:9.

Isaiah 1:18.

Come now, and let us reason together,' says the LORD, 'Though your sins are as scarlet, they will be as white as snow; though they are red like crimson, they will be like wool.

"Sins are as scarlet," "though they are red like crimson."

"Are" not "were" This is once again in the active indicative tense.

If God considers His children "as white as snow" in terms of their iniquities, then how does he warrant the right to still call them sinners?

"Whosoever is born of God doth not commit sin."

Jesus is born of God and we all know that He was and is impeccably sinless. So if we are born again in Christ, we've inherited His perfect, impeccable nature and also the title of that perfection. So anyone that tells you that 1 John 3:9 refers to Christians literally not sinning, they are either lying, deceived about sin or a Biblical Contradictionist. They reach a huge roadblock when going up against:

1 John 1:8.

If we claim to be without sin, we deceive ourselves and the truth is not in us.

Scripture claims that those who are in Christ no longer sin positionally. For it isn't them but the sin inside of them that sins! In God's eyes, those who are in Christ, no longer sin, but these scriptures need to be discerned through the honest, humble lenses of man (acknowledging that we are still sinners in our experience). Because if not, we'd become not only deceived about sin, but arrogant, pious, pharisaical liars!

1 Corinthians 2:14.

The man without the Spirit does not accept the things that come from the Spirit of God, for they are foolishness to him, and he cannot understand them, because they are spiritually discerned.

Jeremiah 31:34.

And they shall teach no more every man his neighbour, and every man his brother, saying, Know the

LORD: for they shall all know me, from the least of them unto the greatest of them, saith the LORD: for I will forgive their iniquity, and I will <u>remember their sin no more</u>.

Jeremiah 50:20.

In those days, and in that time, saith the LORD, the iniquity of Israel shall be sought for, and there shall be none; and the sins of Judah, and they shall not be found: for I will pardon them whom I reserve.

What an amazing verse. It exemplifies the idea of: "what sin?"

It says that no sins will be found. That is not because Israel was sinless. It is however because their sins are all pardoned and paid for by the precious blood of our Saviour and Lord Jesus Christ.

God bless.

4.Believe only.

Jesus is the Saviour of the world. (1 Timothy 4:10. 1 John 2:2. John 3:16. 2 Corinthians 5:14-15. Isaiah 45:22.)

Matthew 18:11.

For the Son of man is come to save that which was lost.

Luke 9:56.

For the Son of man is not come to destroy men's lives, but to save them. And they went to another village.

Salvation however is only attained by faith or believing in Jesus for eternal life. As we've seen in a plethora of scriptures believing is enough! A onetime act of believing. It is important that I keep emphasizing this for so many people think that continual faith is part of salvation. It is not. (Ephesians 1:13.)

Luke 8:12.

Those by the way side are they that hear; then cometh the devil, and taketh away the word out of their hearts, lest they should believe and be saved.

"Believe and be saved!" Pretty clear.

Luke 7:50.

And he said to the woman, Thy <u>faith</u> hath <u>saved</u> thee; go in peace.

This is salvation by faith alone.

This salvation is also instantaneous. Look at the following verses.

Luke 18:42-43. And Jesus said unto him, Receive thy sight: thy <u>faith hath saved thee.</u> And immediately he received his sight, and followed him, glorifying God: and all the people, when they saw it, gave praise unto God.

Receiving sight is analogous to being eternally saved. Look at the instantaneousness of such a reception of this eternal life. *Immediately he received his sight.* As I've belabored, salvation is a onetime, one shot event! That's good news.

Mark 5:34-36.

And he said unto her, Daughter, thy <u>faith</u> hath <u>made thee whole</u>; go in peace, and be whole of thy plague. While he yet spake, there came from the ruler of the synagogue's house certain which said, Thy daughter is dead: why troublest thou the Master any further? As soon as Jesus heard the word that was spoken, he saith unto the ruler of the synagogue, Be not afraid, <u>only believe</u>.

Luke 8:48-50. *And he said unto her, Daughter, be of good comfort: thy <u>faith</u> hath <u>made thee whole</u>; go in peace. While he yet spake, there cometh one from the ruler of the synagogue's house, saying to him, Thy daughter is dead; trouble not the Master. But when Jesus heard it, he answered him, saying, Fear not: <u>believe only</u>, and she shall be <u>made whole</u>.*

Made whole is analogous to saved. And it is simply by believing in Jesus. So, yes, believing is enough to be eternally saved and secure in Christ. John reiterates this point dozens of times in the Gospel of John. (John 1:12, 3:15-16, 18, 36, 6:40, 47, 11:25-26.)

John 20:30-31.

And many other signs truly did Jesus in the presence of his disciples, which are not written in this book: But these are written, that ye might <u>believe</u> that Jesus is the Christ, the Son of God; and that <u>believing</u> ye might have life through his name.

So simple is the gospel. Just believe in Jesus for the free gift of eternal life that can never be lost.

God bless.

5.Impartation Versus Imputation.

1 Corinthians 15:1.

Moreover, brethren, I declare unto you the gospel which I preached unto you, which also ye have received, and wherein ye stand.

The doctrines of <u>Impartation</u> and <u>Imputation.</u>

This is the doctrinal splitter. The very line of demarcation drawn. The dichotomy. These two doctrines determine everything.

Eternal Security versus Conditional Salvation.

Lordship Salvation versus Free Grace.

Sola Fide versus Faith plus Works.

Which one is it going to be? Can't have both. Imputation or Impartation.

Here, I will critique both doctrines.

The Doctrine Of Impartation.

The doctrine of impartation is the idea that once we are saved, Christ has imparted His righteousness to us. In other words, He's given us the ability to be righteous and then we are expected to retain righteousness through our own works. This doctrine doesn't work. We all know that Christ never sinned. We all know that we sin all the time!

If Christ imparted us His righteousness we would be perfect just like Him. But we know that that's not true.

Romans 3:28.

For all have sinned, and come short of the glory of God.

Since we know that we are not perfect, the idea that the imparted righteousness of Christ must mean that we are to strive to be perfect. But scripture says that that is impossible. In fact, through our own self-perception of perfection, we'd all be made liars. You read it in the last subset, now read it again. In fact read this verse until it is memorized.

1 John 1:8.

If we say that we have no sin, we deceive ourselves, and the truth is not in us.

So now what we have is a double paradox. It's impossible to be righteous and if we try we become a liar, which reverses and cancels out our righteousness. So when Christ imparted unto us His righteousness he must have given us a righteousness tainted by sin. Now we've got a triple paradox.

Sinful righteousness, come on!

Isaiah 64:6.

But we are all as an unclean thing, and all our righteousnesses are as filthy rags; and we all do fade as a leaf; and our iniquities, like the wind, have taken us away.

So Christ must have sinned if He has given us His righteousness in which we — after having been imparted — still exhibit sinfulness. This also must mean that God is unrighteous. That contradicts the following scripture.

Romans 9:14.

What shall we say then? Is there unrighteousness with God? God forbid.

This is an attack on Christ's character and is pure heresy! That is, if we strove to be perfect as God requires us.

Matt 5:48.

Be ye therefore perfect, even as your Father which is in heaven is perfect.

That means that after being imparted Christ's righteousness if we slipup one time we have failed and Christ has to die all over again. To think otherwise is to redefine what "perfect" means. The doctrine of impartation is decidedly false.

Here's an example why the doctrine of impartation is perilous, erroneous and for the unsaved that try to practice it, damnable! Christ supposedly gave us or imparted to us His righteousness but it's up to us to <u>keep</u> it. If WE keep it, it becomes <u>our</u> righteousness or self-righteousness. Scripture addresses and refutes this nonsense.

Romans 10:3.

For they being ignorant of God's righteousness, and going about to establish their <u>own</u> <u>righteousness</u>, have <u>not</u> submitted themselves unto the righteousness of God.

See, trying to keep your imparted righteousness is what the Bible calls "ignorant." Ignorant it is and so is the doctrine of impartation.

The Doctrine Of Imputation.

What does impute mean? Let's ask our dictionary.

(To attribute (righteousness, guilt, etc.) to a person or persons vicariously, ascribe as derived from another.)

The archaic and obsolete definition as from Bible times defined it as: To charge (a person) with a fault.

That's what Adam did when he ate of the forbidden fruit. He imputed sin unto the world.

Romans 5:12-13.

Wherefore, as by one man sin entered into the world, and death by sin; and so death passed upon all men, for that all have sinned: For until the law sin was in the world: but sin is not imputed when there is no law.

It is Christ who imputed righteousness back into His believers.

Romans 5:17.

For if by one man's offence death reigned by one; much more they which receive abundance of grace and of the gift of righteousness shall reign in life by one, Jesus Christ.

The Greek word for "impute" is: *Logizomai.*

Which means to reckon or account for. When we are saved and imputed Christ's righteousness, this means that our record of sins, past, present, future, is wiped clean and His spotless record is accounted for us. Hence making us righteous by position, not by behavior. We all know that we are as wicked as can be even in our most self-righteous state. (Psalm 39:5)

The only way we could be considered righteous was if it were imputed or accounted to us through Christ.

In other words, we may see ourselves as being sinners, but God as our judge doesn't. He sees us as spotless and blameless. Just as He sees Christ. God, the father on the other hand, still sees us as sinful in order to discipline and chastise us. He works with us as any good paternal father would with his children. God the judge, who exonerated us on Calvary, cannot see us as sinful, because that was justified when Christ said:

"It is finished."

If there will ever be a time when God turns His back on us for being sinners, it was 2000 years ago. The words: "It is finished (Tetelastai … *paid in full*)" means that He will never turn His back on us again. He has no need to. You don't finish something just to restart it or refinish it for that matter. If it had to be refinished, then it was never really finished in the first place. This is what the doctrine of imputation guarantees us. This is the good news. This is why God is good! To believe in anything contrary to this is a false teaching.

Here are some more scriptures on imputed righteousness.

Romans 4:11. 2 Corinthians 5:19-21. Romans 4:8. Romans 4:22-24. Job 29:14. Isaiah 50:17. Galatians 2:21.

6.Abiding In Christ.

John 15:4.

Abide in me, and I in you. As the branch cannot bear fruit of itself, except it abide in the vine; no more can ye, except ye abide in me.

What does "abide" mean? To act in accord with. Or to submit to. We all know that Christians don't always and in most cases (never) act in accord to God's will or submit to Christ.

What this is saying is that when you <u>abide in Christ,</u> or submit to Him, worship Him, pray to Him, live in the spirit, at that very moment you are not sinning.

1 John 3:6.
Whosoever abideth in him <u>sinneth not</u>: whosoever sinneth hath not seen him, neither known him.

This is not talking about Christians never sinning. Rather, it is talking about Christians that are <u>abiding</u> <u>in</u> <u>Christ</u> or giving Christ their time: I.e., prayer, Bible reading, musical worship, fellowship, etc, … etc. At that time of <u>abiding</u> <u>in</u> <u>Christ</u>, you are not sinning. Whosoever sinneth hath not seen him, neither known him. This is saying that those who live in sin, or don't abide in Christ, don't know Him. This is not talking about salvation. Knowing God is about maturity.

John 14:9.

Jesus saith unto him, Have I been so long time with you, and yet hast thou not <u>known</u> me, Philip? He that seen me hath seen the Father; and how sayest thou then. Shew us the Father?

Philip was a disciple and Jesus said that he didn't know Him. The best analogy I can think of would be an unknown girl calling me up with a sweet, tantalizing voice. She asks me out and I take a chance and say "yes." If she turns out to be trouble I can always undo my action. If someone were to ask me if I were going out with her, I'd say yes but if they asked me if I knew her, I'd have to say: "no, … not really."

So this verse is not talking about a Christian who doesn't ever sin. This is talking about a Christian who isn't consistently living right (abiding in Christ). When you're not abiding in Christ; you are <u>sinning</u>. Some may be wondering what this sin is. The sin is "not abiding in Christ," — in and of itself.

An example would be. Putting your Bible down, picking up the TV remote control and indulging in a half hour of Cable TV. During this crude, carnal, slapstick hilarity, you were not abiding in Christ. So, for a half-an-hour you have sinned! According to this verse.

When we abide in Christ, we are at that moment, not sinning. Pretty simple to understand if we could just infuse spiritual intelligence with scriptural discernment.

In roughshod laymen terms. I'll explain this further. As a Christian, we (try to) walk in the Spirit. But let's say that a Christian gets peevishly frustrated because his girlfriend cheated on and dumped him. In the heat of this vehement anger, he decides to go out and live in selfish, pleasurable sin.

He is, at that period of debauchery, not <u>abiding in Christ</u>, therefore, grossly sinning. When he finally gets his head on straight and repents — comes home if you will, renewing his prayer life and reading his Bible again, he is then <u>abiding in Christ</u> and therefore not sinning — at that very moment!

Chiasm. If you are abiding in Christ, you're not sinning, if you are sinning, you are not abiding in Christ. Fortunately, this has nothing to do with salvation. Titus 3:5-7. Romans 9:11. Romans 4:5. Ephesians 2:8-9. 2 Timothy 1:9.

God bless.

7. The Cheapening Of Scripture.

It upsets me when people undermine and demean the simple doctrines of free grace or faith alone (Sola fide). It insults and cheapens who God is and makes His love weaker than man's. No father in his right mind would disinherit his own children. But some think that the Giver of life and love, whom loves in an infinite capacity, would do something as morbid as we would. This makes me sick. If God cannot save man based on man's pathetic weakness or lack of legalistic performance, then God is not good. Period!

We might as well just start changing the scriptures to commensurate such an unloving, unkeeping god.

Scripture reads.

Psalm 18:2.

The LORD is my rock, and my fortress, and my deliverer; my God, my strength, in whom I will trust; my buckler, and the horn of my salvation, and my high tower.

If God is as fussy and narrow-minded, legalistic and unforgiving as most make Him out to be, he would say things such as: "you've lost your salvation" or "you weren't good enough to get to heaven" or "you misapplied the scripture and didn't get it right!" or "your doctrine of free grace was a lie and I really wasn't mighty enough to keep you saved with all your horrible sins and disobedience. This concept of God totally negates the abovementioned scripture.

If you believe you can lose your salvation, or if God is unable to forgive certain sins, then let me paraphrase how this scripture should be interpreted on <u>your</u> behalf.

The Lord is my Styrofoam stump, and my fortress built out of sawdust shavings, and my deliverer from only past sins; my god, (lowercase) my feeble strength, in whom I shouldn't trust; my buckler made of cheap straw, and the plastic toy trumpet of my salvation, and my high tower made out of Oreo cookie crumbs.

This is not sacrilegious, because My God is not what this travesty of scripture entails. My God is: my <u>rock</u>, and my <u>fortress</u>, and my <u>deliverer</u>; my <u>God</u>, my <u>strength</u>, in whom I will trust; my <u>buckler</u>, and the <u>horn</u> <u>of</u> <u>my salvation</u>, and my <u>high tower</u>.

Rock = Confidence!

Fortress = Hope!

Deliverer = Savior!

God = Father!

Strength = Power!

Buckler = Protection!

Horn of My salvation = Assurance!

High tower = Whom I look up to!

So how do I know that Sola Fide is true? Simple. If it were not, everyone including myself and you — the reader — would end up in hell!

Psalm 130:3.

If thou Lord, shouldest mark iniquities, O Lord, who shall stand?

This isn't a rhetorical question.

If Sola Fide weren't true, the answer is: NO ONE!

Thank God Sola Fide (Faith alone) is true.

God bless.

8.Who Keeps Whom?

There's a huge debate out there about "who keeps whom." Is it our faith that keeps us saved or is it God's? Extreme Arminians believe that it is our faith, works, deeds, righteousness, etc that keep us in good salvific stead with God. In other words, we must keep ourselves saved. This is not only calling God a liar, it is calling God a loser! Because if we could do anything to no longer remain saved, God would be Little Bo Peep who lost some of His sheep.

John 10:11.

I am the good shepherd: the good shepherd giveth his life for the sheep.

This says that God is a "good shepherd." If a shepherd lost his sheep he wouldn't be a good shepherd, ontologically, professionally or ethically speaking. A shepherd who lost his sheep would be a "bad shepherd" a "mediocre shepherd" a "novice shepherd", or an "unskilled shepherd".

Thinking that God could lose His sheep is calling the Bible a liar.

It is God who keeps us saved and it is His faithfulness that grants us salvation.

Hebrews 10:23.

Let us hold fast the profession of our faith without wavering; (for he is faithful that promised.)

Our faith in Him, (Sola Fide), must be predicated on His faithfulness in keeping us. Picture a marriage. What would be the point in placing trust in your soon-to-be spouse if there was no votive assurance that your spouse would be equally and incessantly faithful to you? The scripture is very clear that God's faith keeps us saved.

Romans 3:3-4.

For what if some did not believe? shall their unbelief make the faith of God without effect? God forbid: yea, let God be true, but every man a liar; as it is written, That thou mightest be justified in thy sayings, and mightest overcome when thou art judged.

1 Corinthians 1:9.

God is faithful, by whom ye were called unto the fellowship of his Son Jesus Christ our Lord.

Psalm 36:5.
Thy mercy, O LORD, is in the heavens; and thy faithfulness reacheth unto the clouds.

1 Peter 4-5.

To an inheritance incorruptible, and undefiled, and that fadeth not away, reserved in heaven for you, Who are <u>*kept*</u> *by the power of God through faith unto salvation ready to be revealed in the last time.*

Jude 1:24.

Now unto him that is able to <u>keep you from falling</u>, and to present you faultless before the presence of his glory *with exceeding joy.*

If you're still not convinced then read the entire 121st Psalm.

For the sake of easily spotting the punctilios of this proof-textual truth, I've not italicized the following verses.

Psalm 121.

I will lift up mine eyes unto the hills, from whence cometh my help. My help cometh from the LORD, which made heaven and earth. He will not suffer thy foot to be moved: he that <u>keepeth</u> thee will not slumber. Behold, he that <u>keepeth</u> Israel shall neither slumber nor sleep. The LORD is thy <u>keeper</u>: the LORD is thy shade upon thy right hand. The sun shall not smite thee by day, nor the moon by night. The LORD shall <u>preserve</u> thee from all evil: he shall <u>preserve</u> thy soul. The LORD shall <u>preserve</u> thy going out and thy coming in from this time forth, and even for evermore.

"Keep" in Greek: *Shawmar*. Guard, protect.

"Preserve" in Greek: *Khawyaw*. To sustain life, to live forever.

I hope this is perfectly clear. God keeps us, not the other way around.

Psalm 37:28.

For the LORD loveth judgment, and forsaketh not

his saints; they are preserved for ever: but the seed of the wicked shall be cut off.

It isn't our faith that keeps us saved: it is God's faithfulness.

2 Thessalonians 3:3.

But the Lord is faithful, and he will strengthen and protect you from the evil one.

God bless.

9.Willful Sins!

Beware of Conditional Salvationists, OSFs, heretics, fakes, and scripturally impaired people that undermine the doctrine of Sola Fide with these misunderstood verses. I find that people use Hebrews10:26-27 quite often to condemn habitual sinners, which conversely elevates them to some lofty pedestal, which ironically is a willful sin. And the Bible clearly warns us not to go there.

Romans 12:3.

For I say, through the grace given unto me, to every man that is among you, not to think of himself more highly than he ought to think; but to think soberly, according as God hath dealt to every man the measure of faith.

Hebrews 10:26-27.

For if we sin wilfully after that we have received the knowledge of the truth, there remaineth no more sacrifice for sins. But a certain fearful looking for of judgment and fiery indignation, which shall devour the adversaries.

Does this mean that a true Christian who keeps on sinning willfully has either lost his salvation or was never really saved in the first place? To answer both parts of this question is:

No! No! No! No! No!

First of all it says, "*Received the knowledge of the*

truth."

In other words, the Jews received the gospel of Christ, but refused to believe it for it would supercede and abolish their Old Covenant sacrificial system. They reckoned the blood of the covenant as common and not <u>redemptive</u> and <u>divine</u>. Their willful sin, which was rejecting Christ by the way, was insulting the spirit of grace. People who had received the knowledge of truth and either never believed or stopped believing it committed this apostasy. Verse 29 confirms this where it says: and hath counted the blood of the covenant, wherewith he was sanctified, an unholy thing, and hath done despite unto the spirit of grace?

This was the willful sin.

If this portion of scripture was speaking of sin in its generality, then such sins as: gossip, smoking cigarettes, neglecting to read the Bible, laziness, cussing, carelessness and many other sins could be considered unpardonable sins.

I've never viewed someone that was willfully smoking a cigarette as counting the Blood of Christ unholy. He's killing his lungs and making a fool of himself by coughing profusely, but no, his sin is not the "willful sin" these verses speak of.

They are speaking of apostasy, lapsing into Judaism.

The author of Hebrews, and I believe the Bible

supports this through-and-through, is not implying here that true Christians are committing apostasy! Apostasy is something that the church (i.e., Laodicea, Rome, Pergamos) in the mise-en-scene sense is gradually devolving into.

Picture a church that started out with true believers but after so many years: legalists, hypocrites, false teachers and Pharisees creep in unaware. The true believers become wise to this apostasy and began leaving piecemeal. After so many years, all the church has left is apostates that never truly believed in Christ in the first place.

Hebrews 10:39, asserts that true believers aren't becoming individually apostate.

But we are not of them who draw back unto perdition; but of them that believe to the saving of the soul.

Drawing back into perdition would be analogous to apostatizing.

In other words, going back to a system that could not save them, like the animal sacrifices of the old covenant. That was their "willful sin".

The reason it says that there will be a *"fearful looking for of judgment and fiery indignation, which shall devour the adversaries"* is because these Jews had been amply warned and scripture states this when it says: *"received the knowledge of the truth"*.

What this means is that those who have received the truth and still rejected it are going to be dealt a severer punishment. Compare that to:

Matthew 11:22.

But I say unto you, It shall be more tolerable for Tyre and Sidon at the day of judgment, than for you.

And Matthew 11:24.

But I say unto you, That it shall be more tolerable for the land of Sodom in the day of judgment, than for thee.

These verses about "willfully sinning" may not even referring to true born-again Christians because how could someone in their right mind that has authentically come to Christ later deny the blood covenant of His saving grace and furthermore want to recidivate back the old covenant?

So many people who have been disillusioned or who want to poison the message of the gospel will use these verses to condemn someone with an addictive, willful or habitual sin. In doing so, they've deceitfully wrested these verses out of their original context and basically given NO ONE any hope for a secured salvation!

Why?

Because everyone willfully sins! 1 Kings 7:46.

If you think otherwise, then you are willfully being prideful, full of yourself and arrogant. Prideful, self-contained, arrogance leads to boasting and what does the Bible say about boasting?

James 4:16.

But now ye rejoice in your boastings: all such rejoicing is <u>evil.</u>

When man pridefully boasts, not only is he sinning; he is also being EVIL!

What does the Bible say about pride?

James 4:6.

But he giveth more grace. Wherefore he saith, God resisteth the <u>proud</u>, but giveth grace unto the <u>humble</u>.

Humility admits to willfully sinning!

Pride denies it!

God bless.

10.The Simplicity Of Salvation.

Being a Christian is not by any means simple; becoming a Christian however is!

Getting saved is the simplest thing in the world to do! Discipleship is another matter, and I won't go into the intricate details of how arduous that can be at times in this subset. I want to let scripture unveil how simple Sola Fide is by itself.

Psalm 119:130.

The entrance of thy words giveth light; it giveth understanding unto the <u>simple</u>.

Psalm 19:7.

The law of the LORD is perfect, converting the soul: the testimony of the LORD is sure, making wise the <u>simple</u>.

There's a contrast between "wise" and "simple" in a lot of verses. But there's also a difference between childlike simplicity and ignorant simplicity. This verse talks about a person who has become wise from a starting-off standpoint of simplicity. Most biblical translations make it laborious to get this connotation from this exact verse, but the Contemporary English Version (CEV) makes it crystal clear.

Psalm 19:7.

The Law of the LORD is perfect; it gives us new life. His teachings last forever, and they give wisdom to ordinary people.

"Ordinary" is "synonymous" with "simple." God wants us to start out simple in order to be saved by faith alone, but as we grow spiritually, God wants to rear us up as disciples of wisdom.

But it starts out with Spartan simplicity. It must! A friend of mine said to me long ago that Christianity couldn't be true.

Quote…

"It's just too cut-and-dry to be true."

Unquote.

Yeah, aren't you glad?

It needs to be cut-and-dry so that everyone can attain it, simply, by faith alone. Childlike faith! God wants every type of person to be saved. In all walks of life. (Galatians 3:28.)

Revelation 14:6.

I saw another angel. This one was flying across the sky and had the eternal good news to announce to the <u>people</u> of every <u>race</u>, <u>tribe</u>, <u>language</u>, and <u>nation</u> on earth.

With such cross-national, cross-cultural, cross-ethnic diversity, simplicity must be how the gospel is offered and attained. Salvation must be understood through the simple eyes and heart of a child. I'm not saying that children have to understand it soteriologically, because children are already exempt from eternal punishment.

2 Samuel 12:22-23.

And he said, While the child was yet alive, I fasted and wept: for I said, Who can tell whether GOD will be gracious to me, that the child may live? But now he is dead, wherefore should I fast? can I bring him back again? I shall go to him, but he shall not return to me.

King David believed that his child was automatically transmigrated to heaven, for he expressed his sound belief in infant immorality, the child was with God, having passed from this life to the next. And David knew that someday he would die and see his child again. It's really quite simple, all children who die go to heaven without question! But we should still evangelize children because they can believe.

(Mark 9:42, 2 Timothy 3:15, John 3:16.)

Childlike, simplistic faith is our free ticket to heaven!

I've heard so many people say that children and infants won't go to heaven unless they are saved or baptized, suggesting that they may go to hell. I've even heard hyper-Calvinistic people say that God foreknows their fate and in such foreknowledge gives them no chance to escape hell, even if they were to die as a three-year-old!

This is a blasphemously putrid defilement of God's character and His inimitable, agape love!

Calvinism taken to its sickest extreme supports this heretical nonsense. In my not-so humble opinion, anyone who thinks that God has predestined certain, random people to hell — beyond their control — including unbeknownst children needs to be incarcerated. I say this with vehemence!

I was at a hyper-Calvinistic website not too long ago, and the founder of the website wrote a morbidly disgusting poem about "the elect". It was basically a *nah-nah-nuh-boo-boo* bragging session about the elect's fixed salvation, deriding the ineluctable fate of the non-elect as if laughingly boasting that the elect would go to heaven and the non-elect was eternally appointed to hell! This man is a card-carrying devil-worshipper as far as I'm concerned.

It made me sick to my stomach. I literally thought to myself in a fit of indignation, that anyone who holds to this sick, fatalistic, extreme Calvinistic viewpoint, NEEDS TO BE SENT TO THE FUNNY FARM! And I still adhere to this conviction! Calvinism in any of its forms is a departure from the inclusiveness of the gospel message. 2 Peter 3:9.

Matthew 18:1-4.

At the same time came the disciples unto Jesus, saying, Who is the greatest in the kingdom of heaven? And Jesus called a little child unto him, and set him in the midst of them, And said, Verily I say unto you, Except ye be converted, and become as little children, ye shall not enter into the kingdom of heaven. Whosoever therefore shall humble himself as this little child, the same is greatest in the kingdom of heaven.

Mark 9:36-37.

And he took a child, and set him in the midst of them: and when he had taken him in his arms, he said unto them, Whosoever shall receive one of such children in my name, receiveth me: and whosoever shall receive me, receiveth not me, but him that sent me.

Childlike simplicity is very clear in scripture. The OSFs and Conditional Salvationists will have a hard time refuting such verses as…

Psalm 116:6.

The LORD preserveth the simple: I was brought low, and he helped me.

Proverbs 9:4-6.

Whoso is simple, let him turn in hither: as for him that wanteth understanding, she saith to him, Come, eat of my bread, and drink of the wine which I have mingled. Forsake the foolish, and live; and go in the way of understanding.

These scriptures are clear that we start out simple with a simple faith but then we live, grow up and mature into a wise understanding of the Lord.

To deny Sola Fide is to deny salvific simplicity.

2 Corinthians 1:12.

For our rejoicing is this, the testimony of our conscience, that in simplicity and godly sincerity, not with fleshly wisdom, but by the grace of God, we have had our conversation (citizenship) *in the world, and more abundantly to you-ward.*

2 Corinthians 11:3.

But I fear, lest by any means, as the serpent beguiled Eve through his subtilty, so your minds should be corrupted from the <u>simplicity</u> that is in <u>Christ</u>.

This verse should be memorized and the latter part should be reiteratively noted.

Repeat this over and over again.

Simplicity that is in Christ!

Simplicity that is in Christ!

Simplicity that is in Christ!

Simplicity that is in Christ!

Simplicity that is in Christ!

So yes, it is that cut-and-dry!

Sola Fide is so simple. The Bible makes it clear that it is faith alone in Christ alone that saves us and not even much faith. Just simple faith. Mustard seed faith. A moment of faith.

Matthew 17:20.

And Jesus said unto them, Because of your unbelief: for verily I say unto you, If ye have faith as a grain of mustard seed, ye shall say unto this mountain, Remove hence to yonder place; and it shall remove; and nothing shall be impossible unto you.

It's too easy.

Matthew 11:30.

For my yoke is easy, and my burden is light.

If Sola Fide weren't true, then one must institute works into the soteriological hand-basket of salvific requirements.

Matthew 11:30 would have to at least read like this:

For my yoke is easy, and my burden is light work.

Denying Sola Fide in light of this is adding to scripture, as it always does.

Not only is a simple faith easy, but it is also: pure, peaceable, gentle, merciful, fruitful, impartial, and non-hypocritical.

James 3:17.

But the wisdom that is from above is first <u>pure</u>, then <u>peaceable</u>, <u>gentle</u>, and <u>easy</u> to be intreated, <u>full of mercy</u> and <u>good fruits</u>, <u>without partiality</u>, and <u>without hypocrisy</u>.

This means that faith in Christ is simple, easy to be entreated, given to anyone without partiality and hypocrisy. In other words, God is good for His word.

Salvation must be simple otherwise Christ wouldn't have said come to me as a child. He would've said come to me as a Rocket Scientist or as a college graduate or as a doctor with a long train of alphabet soup following his professional title.

The Bible gives no indication that anyone must be of any intellectual status or credence. Nothing could be simpler than:

Genesis 15:6.

And he believed in the LORD; and he counted it to him for righteousness.

John 1:12.

But as many as received him, to them gave he power to become the sons of God, even to them that believe on his name:

John 3:15.

That whosoever believeth in him should not perish, but have eternal life.

God bless.

11.Addictions.

(If you're a Christian with an addiction, this should be music to your ears.)

Alcoholism is in fact an addiction and a sin, but getting drunk does not mean that a person is not saved! It is a sin like all other sins. Alas, there are some so-called Christians that try to malign this sin as if it will keep someone from heaven. Such people don't understand grace and as much as I hate to write this — those that say you must stop drinking to go heaven may very well be lost and on their way to hell! Let me repeat myself. It isn't those that drink who are lost but those who are trying to stop drinking (to be saved) and those who demand one must stop drinking to be saved. Such people I fear are still lost because they haven't let God save them by his amazing grace through simply believing in Jesus Christ for the free gift of eternal life. (John 6:47.)

Let me break this down.

You have three people: three "Joes" — if you will.

1. Joe "drunk."

2. Joe "stopped drinking."

3. Joe "condemns drunks."

Joe "drunk" is saved by God's grace by believing in Jesus alone for his salvation. He wants to stop drinking but can't. He's addicted.

Joe "stopped drinking" believes with all his heart that he is now going to heaven because he gave that habit up! He's not really trusting in Jesus alone for his salvation.

Joe "condemns drunks" hasn't personally trusted in Jesus by faith alone and he preaches behind the pulpit every Sunday that drunkards — despite grace — are on their way to hell. Nobody gets saved by this nonsense I might add.

Now, imagine it is judgment day: God asks all three "Joes" why should I let you into my glorious kingdom?

Joe "stopped drinking," replies with:

Because I stopped drinking and lived a holy life.

Joe "condemns drunks," replies with:

Because I was sober and didn't drink.

Joe "drunk" replies with:

Because I'm a sinner. Jesus was my savior. I believed on Him and your grace saved me entirely.

The first two Joes will hear God say: WRONG ANSWER! Depart from me I never knew you!

Joe drunk, who drank himself to sleep every night will hear God say: COME ON IN — Into everlasting bliss!!!

Why? Because of GRACE!

What about the heretics that try to use scriptures to condemn drunkards.

1 Corinthians 6:10.

Nor thieves, nor covetous, nor drunkards, nor revilers, nor extortioners, shall inherit the kingdom of God.

I will deal with such passages later in the subset, entitled: Biblical Contradictionism. Entrance and inheritance is not the same thing.

Back to the thesis.

An addiction is an addiction!

A sin is a sin!

Everybody has got some kind of addiction, and if they say otherwise they are blinded by the inadvertent addiction of astucious ignorance.

First of all, the consumption of alcohol is not always a sin. The behavior that ensues from such consumption or overconsumption is however a sin resultant of such imbuement.

Mark 7:15.

There is nothing from without a man, that entering into him can defile him: but the things which come out of him, those are they that defile the man.

Drinking alcohol cannot defile anyone, for we are already innately defiled by our Adamic sinful nature. It's the negative effects of the alcohol coming out of a person that produces sin.

Drinking alcohol is not a sin unless the alcohol is fomenting a sinful abnormality in their Christian behavior. I'm not recommending drinking alcohol because it is in my opinion only for certain people with certain physiological and psychological problems. If a man has a headache, give him an aspirin, otherwise stay away from aspirin. Same with alcohol.

Proverbs 31:6-7.

Give strong drink (alcohol) unto him that is ready to perish, and wine unto those that be of heavy hearts. Let him drink, and forget his poverty, and remember his misery no more.

Many Christians will say that alcohol-users are just using alcohol to forget about all their problems. But that's what the Bible says it is for! This isn't a worldly supposition; it is biblical. Read it for yourself! But then you have some that say that alcohol back in the Bible days was non-intoxicating. If that were so, then why would it say: let him drink, and forget his poverty, and remember his misery no more?

When was the last time someone drank apple juice in order to forget his miseries and woes? So, obviously it was strong, fermented and intoxicating.

This does not mean that <u>anybody</u> is allowed to

drink at <u>any given time</u>, but only those who are insomniac, sick, dying, impoverished, depressed and the like. Someone administering an executive company has no right to drink alcoholic beverages. At least not on the job.

Proverbs 31:4.

It is not for kings, O Lemuel, it is not for kings to drink wine; nor for princes strong drink.

Here's a shocker for you!

People need to realize that getting drunk is not always chemically-induced. In fact, I know a lot of teetotalers who according to scripture are drunkards apart from their teetotalism. Drunkenness is out-of-control behavior, crazy, loose, sloppy, licentious, carnal, orgiastic, unstinted, mind-raping madness!

It doesn't even have to be a repercussion to heavy drinking at all.

I've seen people firsthand that I speculated were berserkly drunk, acting as if they were slaphappy, barnyard animals. Cussing, red-faced, obnoxious, loud, and crudely effusive! Punch drunk! I was certain that they were pie-eyed drunk and perma-fried from smoking every type of illicit drug known to man. But a friend of mine informed me that they didn't use drugs or alcohol anymore.

I then concluded that they were <u>drunk-on-Satan</u>. Lost! Godless. Christless! Not even influenced by chemical intoxicants. They were drunk from the liquor of original SIN!

Scripture backs this up.

Isaiah 29:9.

Stay yourselves, and wonder; cry ye out, and cry: they are drunken, but not with <u>wine</u>; they stagger, but not with <u>strong drink</u>.

It's pretty clear that people can be drunk without alcohol!

I'm not condoning alcoholism or drunkenness. Because they are sins! I'm just saying that this is an addiction, no different than any other addiction. For people that say that drunks can't be Christians, look at this verse more analytically.

Ephesians 5:18.

And be not drunk with wine, wherein is excess; but be filled with the Spirit.

This verse proves that Christians can and do get drunk. This verse is an admonition not to drink in excess, but it also says to be filled with the Holy Spirit. Paul is talking to Christians otherwise he wouldn't exhort them to be filled with the spirit. A non-Christian cannot be filled with the spirit. That is impossible for them! Non-Christians live <u>only</u> for the flesh. There's no polarity, no spirit-flesh Ping-Pong match going on in the life of an unbeliever.

Romans 8:8.

So then they that are in the flesh cannot please God.

Mark my words, when you start talking about the Holy Spirit around lost people they will find it to be ludicrous, stupid and undesirable. I know this from firsthand experience.

Another shocker!

Alcohol can be a <u>good</u> thing! But like any other substance; it can be tragically abused.

Think about it:

Anger.

Power.

Medicine.

A kitchen knife.

All can be used for "the good" but also for "the bad." Anger is good if it motivates a protest rally against abortion or euthanasia, but it can be bad if prompting cold-blooded murder. Power can be good but not in the arms of a tyrannous ruler. Medicine is good if it cures the sick, but not if it abets in the suicide of the overdoser. A kitchen knife is good when it cuts a bologna sandwich in half but bad when in the hands of a crazed serial killer.

Alcohol is good if it relieves manic depression, painful tragic memories, insomnia and chronic physical pain before bedtime. But it can also be immoderately and inordinately abused to the point of regretful chagrin!

Peter Kreeft, Catholic philosopher and world-renowned Christian apologist said it best with: (paraphrased.)

"Alcohol was meant to gladden the heart, but if abused it will only sadden the heart."

Psalm 104:15.
And wine that maketh glad the heart of man, and oil to make his face to shine, and bread which strengtheneth man's heart.

Moving on to other addictions.

An addiction is a sin that keeps someone habitual trapped. Constantly sinfully engaged.

Hebrews 12:1.

Wherefore seeing we also are compassed about with so great a cloud of witnesses, let us lay aside every weight, and the sin which doth so easily <u>beset</u> us, and let us run with patience the race that is set before us.

A besetting sin can be an addiction. The word "beset" in Greek is. *Euperistatos.* Meaning: *"Well standing around."*

This is a sin that surrounds us with an advantage over us. A skillful sin that causes an unbelief preventing us from overcoming it. Sounds like an addiction to me.

Romans 7, (whole chapter) is a testimony of addictive sin or sins.

15-25.

For that which I do I allow not: for what I would, that do I not; but what I hate, that do I. If then I do that which I would not, I consent unto the law that it is good. Now then it is no more I that do it, but sin that dwelleth in me. For I know that in me (that is, in my flesh,) dwelleth no good thing: for to will is present with me; but how to perform that which is good I find not. For the good that I would I do not: but the evil which I would not, that I do. Now if I do that I would not, it is no more I that do it, but sin that dwelleth in me. I find then a law, that, when I would do good, evil is present with me.

For I delight in the law of God after the inward man: But I see another law in my members, warring against the law of my mind, and bringing me into captivity to the law of sin which is in my members. O wretched man that I am! who shall deliver me from the body of this death? I thank God through Jesus Christ our Lord. So then with the mind I myself serve the law of God; but with the flesh the law of sin.

So, it is clear that Christians can and do have addictions, even bad ones!

Addictions and Carnal Christians.

I get so sick when I hear sanctimonious

preachers and biblically illiterate people talk about "carnal Christians". I especially hate when they say:

"Listen up, my friend. There's no such thing as a carnal Christian!"

That statement is calling the Word of God a liar.

I can make a case for "carnal Christians" in one verse.

Romans 7:14.

For we know that the law is <u>spiritual</u>: but I am <u>carnal</u>, sold under sin.

Only a Christian can know that the law is spiritual.

1 Corinthians 2:13.

Which things also we speak, not in the words which man's wisdom teacheth, but which the <u>Holy Ghost teacheth</u>; comparing spiritual things with spiritual.

We can't know what is spiritual without the Holy Spirit teaching us.

But Romans 7:14 still says that such a person is carnal.

So if anyone tells you that there's no such thing as a carnal Christian, you now no longer have to buy into this self-righteous mumbo-jumbo.

Carnal Christian deniers basically rest their

hope on how they keep the law. Well, Whoopido! Trying to keep the law makes you carnal!

Before Christ, (the true great high priest) superceded Melchisedek, our efforts to obey the law were filthy.

Hebrews 7:16.

Who is made, not after the law of a <u>carnal commandment</u>, but after the power of an endless life.

So even if we keep the law we are still carnal. So a carnal Christian is not only a law-breaker, but also a law-abider if one wants to go by what the Bible says rather than what man arrogantly speculates.

Such people think that they are pure of sin (like the Wesleyans), but the Bible doesn't support this nonsense.

Proverbs 20:9-10.

Who can say, I have made my heart clean, I am pure from my sin?

Divers weights, and divers measures, both of them are alike abomination to the LORD.

What this is saying is that despite our measure of pureness, it is still an abomination unto God without the righteousness only Christ can give us!

Addictions are a terrible thing but there is hope.

But this hope is in God alone.

1 John 4:4.

Ye are of God, little children, and have overcome them: because greater is he that is in you, than he that is in the world.

God bless.

12. Conditional Salvation Refuted!

John 1:17.

For the law was given by Moses, but grace and truth came by Jesus Christ.

Conditional salvation is as silly as can be and in my opinion satanic, but it's out there! There are Christians or "so-called Christians" everywhere that espouse conditional salvation. They'll assault you with a bunch of misinterpreted scriptures that contradict Sola Fide scriptures. They won't deal with the patent contradictions but will instead throw out more misinterpreted verses.

Conditional Salvationists have a do-it-yourself complex. That's a terrible thing to have. They rely on self-righteousness and scripture makes it clear that until they humble themselves and lose that self-affirmed righteousness, they won't be saved!

1 Peter 4:18.

And if the <u>righteous</u> scarcely be saved, where shall the ungodly and the sinner appear?

Conditional Salvation can't deal with the following verses!

Galatians 3:21-25.

Is the law then against the promises of God? God forbid: for if there had been a law given which could have given life, verily righteousness should have been by the law. But the scripture hath concluded all under sin, that the promise by faith of Jesus Christ might be given to them that believe. But before faith came, we were kept under the law, shut up unto the faith which should afterwards be revealed. Wherefore the law was our schoolmaster to bring us unto Christ, that we might be justified by faith. But after that faith is come, we are no longer under a schoolmaster.

If you are still kept under some kind of law as the Conditional/works/lordship Salvationists claim to still be under, it is because you don't have genuine faith in Christ and Him alone.

I'm not saying it, scripture says it: <u>Before faith</u> came, we were kept under the law.

Conditional Salvation is all about keeping ourselves saved by our own works.

That just doesn't work.

Romans 7:8.

(NAS).

But sin, taking opportunity through the commandment, produced in me coveting of every kind; for apart from the Law sin is dead.

Sin was produced by the law. And in this case: "coveting of every kind." Sin would be dead if there weren't a law. The only logical conclusion I can make about those who are so hell-bent about keeping the law is that they unknowingly like sin because that's all the law produces.

Romans 5:20.

Moreover the law entered, that the <u>offence</u> might <u>abound</u>. But where sin abounded, grace did much more abound.

Conditional Salvation is no different than Pharisaism.

The Pharisees wouldn't admit to being sinners.

They just plain outright didn't like sinners.

Luke 5:30.

The Pharisees and their scribes began grumbling at His disciples, saying, "Why do you eat and drink with the tax collectors and sinners?"

A Conditional Salvationist is a modern day Pharisee!

People that don't (or think they don't) have a lot of sins in their life don't love God the way that they should (or at all). Sounds presumptuous. But I'm not saying it; the Bible says it.

Luke 7:47.

Wherefore I say unto thee, Her sins, which are <u>many</u>, are forgiven; for she loved <u>much</u>: but to whom <u>little</u> is forgiven, the same loveth <u>little</u>.

In other words, if little is forgiven on the basis of thinking that there isn't much to forgive, (Pharisees, self-righteous people, Conditional Salvationists) then you don't have the ability to love God the way you should! So what's the solution? Should you go out and sin more so that your love for God will augment?

No!

If we are humble, honest, introspective, transparent, and confessionary, we will know that we have much, much, much to be forgiven thus much-much-much-much-much love for God!

That is why it is important to ask God to examine our hearts.

Psalm 26:2.
Test me, O LORD, and try me, examine my heart and my mind.

Conditional Salvation insults Christ!

If salvation were conditional, then that means that if we don't adhere to such a condition—whatever it may be beyond some wild stretch of the imagination—then we are in a vulnerable position to perish. It would mean that God might still condemn us if we did something wrong: I.e., lost faith, backslid, sinned over and over again, whatever. But that contradicts scripture.

Romans 8:34. (amplified)

Who is there to condemn (us)? Will Christ Jesus (the Messiah), Who died, or rather Who was raised from the dead, Who is at the right hand of God actually pleading as He intercedes for us?

This is a rhetorical question and the answer is:

Not Christ!

Why would a justifier and an intercessor condemn those he has justified and keeps on interceding for? (Hebrews 7:25.)

Conditional Salvationists have to prescribe condemnation where it is not needed. That is, in the future of the believer.

Romans 5:16.

And not as it was by one that sinned, so is the gift: for the judgment was by one to condemnation, but the free gift is of many offences unto justification.

Not all Conditional Salvationists are lost, as it may seem that I've implied. Some espouse this nonsense out of ignorance. Others out of pride or hatred for sinners, self-centeredness or, as I mentioned earlier, the do-it-yourself complex.

I will say this, if you are a Conditional Salvationist, after reading this you will now know it. If in fact you still refuse to abrogate such heresy I would either question whether you really trust Christ for your salvation or at least your motives for being a Christian.

Some people hate the idea of unfruitful Christians getting by with doing nothing for Christ. As do I. It vexes me to no end when Christians don't read their Bible, don't pray and don't attend church. But you have to remember. Such deeds don't determine our salvation; they simply prove and confirm our concern about sanctification and heavenly rewards.

If your motive for hating spiritual fruitlessness in others is for the sake of their spiritual growth, then you are not a Conditional Salvationist. The dangerous line we draw between faith and works must not be ABOUT salvation otherwise we are guilty of heresy.

Faith is what saves us; works are what we should do out of appreciation for being saved. We should do good works because we've got salvation, not in order to get salvation. Conditional Salvation is a perilous, damnable curse. If one wants to express righteous anger at spiritual babedom and fruitlessness, they need to understand that that is an issue of discipleship/sanctification—not salvation! I get so sick of people doing what I call fruit inspecting and then claiming that someone living like the devil is not really saved. Living like the devil is not proof that someone is not saved; it is only proof that someone is not being sanctified. If a person who lives like the devil and then gets saved but continues to live like the devil cannot be saved or stay saved in that devilish state, grace is not grace! Fortunately, true grace gives us a standing no matter how we live.

(1 Peter 5:12. Romans 5:2.)

There's no such thing as Conditional Salvation. There is conditional discipleship. Once someone is saved by faith alone in Christ alone, they are eternally secure. We then must choose whether we want to be a disciple of God.

A disciple will get splendid rewards in heaven.

A saved deadbeat will miss out.

As Christians, we are to be servants of God, but we don't have to be to attain salvation. We are God's friends and servanthood is optional. But if you decide to be a servant of God, you will be blessed.

Galatians 4:7-9.

Wherefore thou art no more a servant, but a son; and if a son, then an heir of God through Christ. Howbeit then, when ye knew not God, ye did service unto them which by nature are no gods. But now, after that ye have known God, or rather are known of God, how turn ye again to the weak and beggarly elements, whereunto ye desire again to be in bondage?

Conditional Salvation is bondage.

And TOTALLY unbiblical!

Romans 4:5.

But to him that worketh not, but believeth on him that justifieth the ungodly, his faith is counted for righteousness.

God bless.

13.Living In Sin.

So many people think they are not saved because they think they "live in sin." Some people may even count their sins daily to see if they've out-sinned their quota, which may hypothetically qualify them as a candidate that lives in sin. There may be some people that go a day without committing a certain type of sin and on that day they feel <u>saved</u> whereas on any other day, they feel <u>lost</u>.

Some may feel that habitual sin means that they "live in sin."

The problem with this conjecture is that sin is sin and no sin or amount of sins is not covered by Christ's all-sufficient, atoning blood if you are a believer.

Psalm 85:2.
Thou hast forgiven the iniquity of thy people, thou hast covered <u>all their sin.</u> Selah.

But then some might ask themselves: "Am I truly a believer?"

What about all this sin or that sin? First of all, sin is only acknowledged by the fact that we have the Holy Spirit in us.

1 Thessalonians 5:19.

Quench not the Spirit.

We quench (subdue, shun, grieve) the spirit by sinning, rebelling against God. The Holy Spirit is like our spiritual sonar. We wouldn't recognize our sins without Him. This is also true as the Holy Spirit knocks on your heart even before getting saved.

Revelation 3:20.

Behold, I stand at the door, and knock: if any man hear my voice, and open the door, I will come in to him, and will sup with him, and he with me.

The Holy Spirit knocks on everyone's door, but if you snub the spirit as an assertion of unbelief, the knocker goes away with the intention of returning later. But for the active believer, the Holy Spirit stays permanently within us to convict, reproach, teach, guide, direct, etc.

So what does it mean to live in sin?

Philippians 1:22.

But if I live on in the flesh, this will mean fruit from my labor; yet what I shall choose I cannot tell.

Christians don't live in sin positionally. Even if they commit continual sins, they don't live in them.

The biggest thing that we need to be mindful of is that when we continue to sin, we are not living but dying, still saved, yes! But physically dying. (Romans 8:13) There is no life (true living) in the believer when he sins. There's only guilt, shame, depression and self-embarrassment. We are alive (truly living) only when we engage in spiritual things.

Scripture clearly states.

Ephesians 2:1.

And you hath he quickened, who were dead in trespasses and sins.

Before we were saved, everyone was spiritually dead in his or her trespasses. But now that we're saved, everyone is dying physically in their trespasses otherwise the idea of immortality would be the logical corollary.

So what's the alternative to being dead in sin? (Which everyone is to some degree.)

The solution is to abide in Christ; He is our safeguard.

1 Samuel 22:23.

Abide thou with me, fear not: for he that seeketh my life seeketh thy life: but with me thou shalt be in safeguard.

The Bible says that as believers we live with God.

Psalm 23:9.

Surely goodness and mercy shall follow me all the days of my life: and I will dwell in the house of the LORD for ever.

Psalm 91:9.

Because thou hast made the LORD, my refuge, the most High, thy habitation.

If we are dwelling in the house of the Lord, we are not living in sin, even though continual sins may seem as though we live in it. That is not the case by title and position. If our behavior aside from our justification meant that we lived in sin, we'd have to keep an abacus and then decide how many sins qualified us a sin-dweller. That would be a legalistic rendition of moral relativism creeping its way into Christendom. For instance, Steve committed 23 mortal sins on Wednesday and 12 venial sins on Thursday. He lived in sin on Wednesday but because of three junctures of abstention on Friday, he only committed sins as opposed to living in them. This is where "sin gauging" becomes silly, fruitless, unbiblical and a mere game of semantical eenie-meanie-minie-moe.

Christians that are saved by faith and declared righteous through Christ don't live in sin despite the number of sins they commit on a daily basis. Otherwise this psalm wouldn't be able to say that the Lord is my *refuge* and thy *habitation*.

Christians sin, no doubt about it, but they don't positionally live in sin even if it may seem that they do. A non-Christian lives in sin because he doesn't have God as his refuge and habitation. So a non-Christian is someone who is not only identified by his sin but whom also "lives in sin." Not because of his sin, but because of his Christless, spiritually dead lostness.

A Christian positionally lives in Christ.

Romans 6:8.

Now if we died with Christ, we believe that we will also <u>live with him</u>.

Someone may leave his home — metaphorically speaking — and go out and sin. But a non-Christian, by this analogue, is spiritually homeless and therefore living in perpetual, sinful dereliction!

So many people try to tally up the amount of sins Christians commit as if they can exceed Christ's forgiveness.

It doesn't matter if you commit one sin or ten trillion, because we are justified by faith, declared righteous and covered of all sins!

Romans 3:22-24.

Even the righteousness of God which is by faith of Jesus Christ unto all and upon all them that believe: for there is <u>no difference</u> (in how many sins you commit). *For all have sinned, and come short of the glory of God.*

Being justified freely by his grace through the redemption that is in Christ Jesus. (Emphasis mine.)

It doesn't matter how much you've sinned or will sin because ALL HAVED SINNED and fall short of the glory.

Even if we feel like we are totally unworthy of salvation, we must hold our hope on the shoulders of this verse.

Romans 5:6.
For when we were yet without strength, in due time Christ died for the <u>ungodly</u>.

I once made the analogy of two baseball teams. Team one made twenty strikeouts. Team two made only twelve strikeouts. Does team one have any more reason to brag and boast about their great strikeout average? No, because if the God-of-Baseball required infinite strikeouts, they both have still fallen terribly short. According to God everyone has fallen short.

Thinking that you have anything to offer God in terms of merit is engendered from pride.

1 Timothy 6:4.

He is proud, knowing nothing, but doting about questions and strifes of words, whereof cometh envy, strife, railings, evil surmisings.

That's pretty self-explanatory.

The Bible is full of Christians that continued to sin.

1 Corinthians 5:11.

But now I have written unto you not to keep company, if any man that is called a brother be a fornicator, or covetous, or an idolator, or a railer, or a drunkard, or an extortioner; with such an one no not to eat.

Such sinners were called brothers, still saved,

but ostracized from formal worship. Not eternally lost!

Some people try to argue that the sinner here was not really a true-blue brother. But according to the concordance he was.

"Called," (Greek) *Onomazo*: in this verse alone means to: name or to assign an appellation.

An appellation is an official title or designation not a cognomen or false moniker. So these were true Christians committing heinous sins that were to be excommunicated from the church until they repented and used 1 John 1:9.

They were not to be condemned to hell but chastised so that reunion of fellowship was possible.

The big thing that we have to remember about justification is that we are declared righteous. Our true state of righteousness or total sinlessness is yet to come.

Galatians 5:5.

For we through the Spirit <u>wait</u> for the hope of righteousness by faith.

I'm not condoning sin. Don't read this and get all happy and then go out and sin. True messages of grace will tempt the hearer to want to go out and sin at first. But we need to remember what the price of our redemption cost Christ. When I read Brennan Manning's Ragamuffin Gospel for the first time, I was tempted to sin more insensitively. But after reading it for the second time, that caprice wasn't present.

So read this and get all happy over the fact that you have been forgiven and that God is good because of such total forgiveness. Sin does not pay. Sin stinks! I know some goody-goody legalist is going to read this and then say that I'm a false teacher giving a license for immorality. I'm not. Sin committed by Christians is a recipe for deep-seated misery and chastisement. I don't recommend it!

We need to be remindful that there were many true believers in the Bible that committed all sorts of putrid sins. If you think that you are a terrible sinner, trust me there is someone in the Bible who has out-sinned you!

Take a look at.

1 Corinthians 10:1-11.

I will underline each sin these Christians were committing, but take a look at the first verse.

1 — *Moreover, brethren, I would not that ye should be ignorant, how that all our fathers were* under the cloud, and all passed through the sea.

Paul commences with "brethren."

In Greek brethren is *delphus*. In this context it is referring to believers, disciples or fellow Christians. Verse two corroborates this point.

2 — *And were all <u>baptized</u> unto Moses in the cloud and in the sea.*

If they weren't Christians, why would they have been baptized, which means, "identified in Christ" in this passage? (*Baptizo*)

3 — *And did all eat the same spiritual meat.*

If they weren't true Christians then why would the meat be considered spiritual? Spirituality to a non-believer is either: satanic, occultic, silly, foreign or nonexistent.

4 — *And did all drink the same spiritual drink: for they drank of that spiritual Rock that followed them: and that Rock was Christ.*

They drank the rock of Christ.

5 — *But with many of them God was not well pleased: for they were overthrown in the wilderness.*

Here's where it gets indicative that they were terribly sinning.

6 — *Now these things were our examples, to the intent we should not <u>lust after evil things</u>, as they also <u>lusted</u>.*

Not only did they lust, but they lusted after "evil things."

Verse 10:13 talks about how nobody is tempted in a manner that is uncommon to man. Some Christians feel that their lust is damningly more erotic than others, i.e., homoerotic, pedophilic, bestial, vampiric or sadomasochistic. They feel that they can't be saved because their lust-type is too hellish. Lust is lust and sin is sin! Period. If you think that your lust-type is too obscene to be forgiven, just back up to verse 6 and remember that these Corinthian Christians lusted after evil things!

7 — *Neither be ye idolaters, as were some of them; as it is written, The people sat down to eat and drink, and rose up to play.*

8 — *Neither let us commit fornication, as some of them committed, and fell in one day three and twenty thousand.*

Twenty thousand fornicators. That's quite a lot.

9 — *Neither let us tempt Christ, as some of them also tempted, and were destroyed of serpents.*

These people were tempting Christ and were physically destroyed by serpents.

10 — *Neither murmur ye, as some of them also murmured, and were destroyed of the destroyer.*

Murmur in Greek: *gogguzo*. To "mumble", "groan" or "complain."

11 — *Now all these things happened unto them for examples: and they are written for our admonition, upon whom the ends of the world are come.*

Paul didn't write this to reap scorn upon them

in a manner of eternal condemnation; he wrote this to admonish them. So it is clear that these were true believers committing all sorts of heinous sins and some were dying physically because of it. This is good news to the humble and bad news to the proud.

No matter what we do as Christians, we are still eternally <u>saved</u>, but however not always physically <u>safe</u>. Some Christians have a problem with other Christians that are in what they call gross sin. But they take this problem to an ignorant extreme when putting one's salvation on the line.

The extreme Calvinist, who asserts that a true believer will prove his salvation by his lack of sin, will have a sticky wicket of a problem with the above verses.

We should have a problem with our brothers that are sinning grossly. In my opinion the grossest sins are, viz: pride, not attending church, leaving your Bible the way you received it—unopened, and not admitting to having a sin problem which morbidly may justify why you don't go to church, read your Bible or even get saved! But that's just my opinion.

As Christians, we are baptized into one unitary body.

1 Corinthians 12:13.

For by one Spirit are we all baptized into one body, whether we be Jews or Gentiles, whether we be bond or free; and have been all made to drink into one Spirit.

So if you think that you don't have a sin problem, but your brother does, his sin is infecting the very body you are a part of. So whoopidoo if you don't (think you) sin. This is why we should admonish in kindness and not scornfully judge one another and most of all why we should humbly admit that we all sin and are saved ONLY by grace through faith alone in Christ alone!

Think about it!

Put on your thinking cap.

You have two people here.

(Sinner A.)

(Sinner B.)

Sinner A has sinned <u>once</u> in his entire life. Just once!

Sinner B has sinned 25,000,000,000 times.

Who's guiltier?

Without Christ, both are indistinguishably just as guilty as the other and likewise hell-bound.

But with Christ, both are equally justified and totally forgiven!

God bless.

14.Eternally Secure.

Job 11:18.

And thou shalt be <u>secure</u>, because there is hope; yea, thou shalt dig about thee, and thou shalt take thy rest in safety.

One of the biggest and most controversial issues in Christianity is the OSAS (once saved, always saved) issue. I will say that much hypocrisy is found in such discussions on both sides of the argument. Most of it eventuates from subjectivism, traditionalism, and extremism. Some proponents are saying that if you're saved then you'll prove it by your actions. (Calvinists) Others are saying that if you're not proving it by your actions, that is bearing fruit, then you can lose salvation. (Arminians) They would have to change the initialism from OSAS to OTSAS. Once <u>Truly</u> Saved, Always Saved.

If you believe in Jesus Christ for salvation, you are saved. God's word declares this but some may still doubt.

2 Peter 1:10.

Wherefore the rather, brethren, give diligence to make your calling and election sure: for if ye do these things, ye shall never fall.

Your election is certain but we can lose sight of it if we live carnal and lethargic lives. This scripture is talking about how we can have more eternal assurance by the way we live. "Fall," here in Greek is *ptaoi* which means to stumble in sin or unbelief. It has nothing to do with falling from grace or losing your salvation.

Some of the rumors about this doctrine are...

***It gives man a license for immorality.*

***Someone could be saved and then become a devil worshipper.*

***It causes careless living and gives the Christian no reason for diligence.*

***It renders grace an imprimatur for sinlessness, lawlessness and antinomianism.*

I've heard many, many more rumors that I won't list. But it doesn't matter, because these rumors are childish, scripturally ungrounded and erroneous. If a person is truly saved and loves God, he shouldn't want a license for immorality (but sadly some do), nor should he want to convert to Satanism. These are strawman arguments taken to their extreme. When's the last time you heard of a true Christian becoming a devil worshipper?

The doctrine of eternal security is as biblically sound as any other true doctrine. In order to refute it; one must dishonestly twist the scriptures out of their original context thus applying eisegesis rather than exegesis.

Exegesis: A critical explanation or interpretation of a text or portion of a text, especially of the Bible.

Eisegesis: An interpretation, especially of Scripture, that expresses the interpreter's own ideas, biases, or the like, rather than the factual meaning of the text.

A common example of eisegesis is found in the critiquing of this verse.

John 10:29.

My Father, which gave them me, is greater than all; and no man is able to pluck them out of my Father's hand.

"Nobody can pluck you out of God's hand, but you can jump out," they say with smugness.

The ones saying this have to or WANT to believe this in order to support their false doctrine of works salvation. First of all, imagine metaphorically, a wild onion plucking itself out of the ground. Wouldn't that liken to jumping out? So if you can jump out of God's hand, you are calling God a lair. Because it says no man—that includes yourself—you are a man aren't you? It also says that God is greater than all! By saying that you can jump out of God's hands is implying that you and your jumping skills are greater than God or God's ability to keep hold of His own children. Would an earthly father tell one of his children?

"I'll hold unto you and protect you, but if you

want to jump out of my grip … go right on ahead."

No loving father would even begin to think in such a way. This is more proof that the anti-eternal securist doesn't understand the nature of God's *agape* love!

I could see how someone might be able to split semantic hairs with the word "pluck." Obviously God's hand must've been open evoking that the act of plucking could be achievable, like plucking a potato chip shard from someone's hand. But take a look at other versions of the Bible. The word "pluck" is supplanted with "snatch." For someone to snatch you out of God's hand would be much more difficult. So this denotes that God is holding His believers in a closed, steadfast fist. Thus giving us full eternal security. Honestly, can you jump out of a closed hand?

I know that I'm proving my point with hyperbole, but there are lots of objectors out there that will argue this until blue in the face. If they still want to argue, here's another analogy. Let's say that a person has a pet hamster. And they've secured the hamster's cage so that no predacious creatures may harm the defenseless animal. If the pet owner would secure such a cage, why would he leave a way for the hamster to jump out? To think that any human could just jump, like a frog, out of God's hand is to think very small about God's hand hence thinking very small of God.

I don't know about you but even if I were

Michael Jordan, I don't think I could jump out of God's hand! Taking the scripture in wholesale context assures us that both Jesus and the Father's hands are securely holding you. That's double assurance.

Another verse the anti-Eternal Securists might use to refute this doctrine is.

Ezekiel 3:20.

Again, When a righteous man doth turn from his righteousness, and commit iniquity, and I lay a stumbling-block before him, he shall die: because thou hast not given him warning, he shall die in his sin, and his righteousness which he hath done shall not be remembered; but his blood will I require at thine hand.

The word die in Hebrew is *Muwth*. It literally means: "to die", and according to the concordance, a "physical death."

Take a look at:

1 Corinthians 5:4-5.

In the name of our Lord Jesus Christ, when ye are gathered together, and my spirit, with the power of our Lord Jesus Christ, To deliver such an one unto Satan for the destruction of the flesh, that the <u>*spirit may be saved in the day of the Lord Jesus.*</u>

Physical death. Destruction of the flesh, not the spirit. If you keep on sinning as this man was, Satan may take you out of the world physically, but your spirit will still be saved.

The following verse has the same connotation.

John 8:21.

Then said Jesus again unto them, I go my way, and ye shall seek me, and shall die in your sins: whither I go, ye cannot come.

Once again this means to die physically according to the concordance.

There's maturity in believing eternal security.

I find, in most cases, that those who deny eternal security are relatively young in the faith, immature, arrogant, stubborn, lost or just plumb deceived. Anyone who denies eternal security is a Works-Based Salvationist.

All!

Without exception.

If you could do something to lose your salvation; then it would take work of some kind in order to keep from doing this. Even our faithfulness is a form of work. I've called the deniers of eternal security, young, immature, arrogant, stubborn, lost and deceived, but let's take a look at what the Apostle Paul called them.

Galatians 3:1-5.

O <u>foolish</u> Galatians, who hath bewitched you, that ye *should not obey the truth, before whose eyes Jesus Christ hath been evidently set forth, crucified among you? This only would I learn of you, Received ye the Spirit by the works of the law, or by the hearing of faith? Are ye so foolish? having begun in the Spirit, are ye now made perfect by the flesh? Have ye suffered so many things in vain? if it be yet in vain. He therefore that ministereth to you the Spirit, and worketh miracles among you, doeth he it by the works of the law, or by the hearing of faith?*

Paul is calling them foolish.

But there are some that will say that you can't lose your salvation, but you can give it back. Scripture denies this as well. And I will touch on this point in subsequent subsets.

2 Chronicles 19:7.

Wherefore now let the fear of the LORD be upon you; take heed and do it: for there is no iniquity with the LORD our God, nor respect of persons, nor taking of gifts.

God does not take bribes.

You didn't have to do anything to be saved.

You can't do anything to stay saved.

You can't give God your salvation back!

Salvation is a gift.

Romans 6:23.
For the wages of sin is death; but the gift of God is

eternal life through Jesus Christ our Lord.

Salvation is a gift God won't take back.

Romans 11:29.

For the gifts and calling of God are without repentance.

For more clarity, read it from the NIRV.

Romans 11:29.

God does not take back his gifts. He does not change his mind about those he has chosen.

But what about those that willfully leave God?

If their departure was blissful and without regret and then life thereafter was happy-happy-joy-joy, they probably were never truly saved in the first place!

1 John 2:19.

They went out from us, but they were not of us; for if they had been of us, (Once saved) *they would no doubt have continued with us:* (Always saved) *but they went out, that they might be made manifest that they were not all of us.*

If they left God or the faith for some sort of tenable reason, like for instance, the loss of a loved one or anger towards God for allowing so much worldwide evil to exist, and if they were really saved, then they will live miserably and remain in that misery until they use 1 John 1:9. They will undergo a void in their life—which only God can fill. If this is the case, they haven't left Christ at all. Nobody is closer to Christ than those that are gravely suffering.

Philippians 3:10.

That I may know him, and the power of his resurrection, and the fellowship of his sufferings, being made conformable unto his death.

It perturbs me when people claim to be "saved," but don't feed themselves with God's word, don't pray, don't attend church, sin without contrition and yet are as happy as a lark. If such a person is really saved they are awaiting divine chastisement. Hebrews 12.

John 10:27.
My sheep hear my voice, and I know them, and they follow me.

If someone is not doing anything for God; then they are not listening to Him.

God is whispering in a still small voice: … *go to church, … pray … read the Bible … abide in me … go soul-winning … be miserable and feel empty if you refuse to do such things.*

John 10:27 is in fact a verse that guarantees eternal security for the believer, but the Bible does say that there will be people that will receive little if any heavenly rewards—however they still will be saved.

1 Corinthians 3:15.

If any man's work shall be burned, he shall suffer loss: but he himself shall be saved; yet so as by fire.

All I'm saying is that the person professing to being saved but showing no evidence should question whether or not he is in fellowship with God. It is not for us to do. No sin can separate us from God's love. Romans 8:39. But what about if we keep on sinning? Won't that cause us to lose salvation? No.

Psalm 32:1-2.

Blessed is he whose transgression is <u>forgiven</u>, whose <u>sin</u> is covered. Blessed is the man unto whom the LORD imputeth not iniquity, and in whose spirit there is no guile.

Notice it doesn't say "sins". That may leave a skeptic with the inquiry of "what sins". Past, present or future. But it says <u>sin</u>, singular. Meaning the state that we are in, which is undoubtedly sinful. Not only are our sins covered, past, present and future, but the Blood of the Lamb covers our sinful condition as well.

Now moving on to some eternal security proof-texts.

1 Peter 4:19.

Wherefore let them that suffer according to the will of God commit the keeping of their souls to him in well doing, as unto a faithful Creator.

This is talking about totally committing yourself to the fact that God has faithfully saved you. Denying eternal security is to put your salvific trust in something other than God. Like purity, faith-in-self, church, rituals, works, human strength which scripture refutes.

John 15:5.

I am the vine, ye are the branches: He that abideth in me, and I in him, the same bringeth forth much fruit: for without me ye can do nothing.

Mark 14:38.

Watch ye and pray, lest ye enter into temptation. The spirit truly is ready, but the flesh is weak.

More eternal security verses.

Isaiah 49:14-16.

But Zion said, The LORD hath forsaken me, and my Lord hath forgotten me. Can a woman forget her sucking child, that she should not have compassion on the son of her womb? yea, they may forget, yet will I not forget thee. Behold, I have graven thee upon the palms of my hands; thy walls are continually before me.

A child of God hath not to worry about God eternally forsaking them. The latter part of this triplet of scripture says that we are graven or "carved" upon the palms of God's hands. What more eternal security do we need? How does an indention remove itself from what it is etched upon?

Plus, God has fortified us with His walls of continual security.

Colossians 1:13.

Who hath delivered us from the power of darkness, and hath translated us into the kingdom of his dear Son.

Translated in Greek is: *Methistemi.* Which means, to exchange, to transfer, or to remove from one place to another.

When we are saved, our salvation is translated from this life to heaven. I don't think man can fall from heaven back to earth. Losing your salvation in light of this verse is making an erroneous claim.

Saved But Living In Unbelief.

Hebrews 3:8-12.

Harden not your hearts, as in the provocation, in the day of temptation in the wilderness: When your fathers tempted me, proved me, and saw my works forty years. Wherefore I was grieved with that generation, and said, They do alway err in their heart; and they have not known my ways. So I sware in my wrath, They shall not enter into my rest. Take heed, brethren, lest there be in any of you an evil heart of unbelief, in departing from the living God.

When it talks about these wilderness Christians not entering into my rest, it is talking about the rest of

Canaan. Rest in Greek is *katapausis*, meaning repose or peace from receiving God's provision. This is not talking about salvation. That rest is *mnuchah* meaning "resting place."

Unbelief, sin, living in the wilderness, which are all prevalent human conditions for Christians even today will keep you from entering into true rest. Which is the joy of Christian living, being in peace with God. It takes faith or belief — I use the terms interchangeably — to be saved and it takes subsequent faith or belief to enter into the rest of Canaan. That is true peace with God due to fellowship and obedience.

This whole idea that a Christian is saved one day and then lost on another day is not only ridiculous, but also unbiblical.

Matthew 7:23.

And then will I profess unto them, I never knew you: depart from me, ye that work iniquity.

If we can be saved, that is to know Christ wherein He knows us; then this scripture would have to be removed or changed into:

And then will I profess unto them, (I knew you but then I stopped knowing you because you fell away, I got to know you again but you sinned your way out of my grace:) depart from me, ye that work iniquity.

The scripture says: I NEVER knew you.

If you were once saved, then Jesus knew you. Therefore you are always saved. To deny this is to prefer my heretical scripture alteration to the infallible Word of God.

Where does our faith come from?

Faith comes from God. The Bible says that:

Hebrews 12:2.

Looking unto Jesus the author and finisher of (our) faith; who for the joy that was set before him endured the cross, despising the shame, and is set down at the right hand of the throne of God.

If Jesus finishes our faith, it isn't up to us maintain it. This verse is however a paradigm for us to endure in faith and sometimes the only way to do so is to trust that He is the author and finisher of faith and full of faith, whereas we lack. But whether we endure in faith or not has nothing to do with our salvation and we must remember that God is the one who gives us faith.

1 Peter 1:21.

Who by <u>him</u> (God) do believe in God, that raised him up from the dead, and gave him glory; that your faith and hope might be in God.

Psalm 143:1.

Hear my prayer, O LORD, give ear to my supplications: in thy <u>faithfulness</u> answer me, in thy righteousness.

We may exercise some faith, but God is "full of faith".

Is the concept of eternal security in the Bible?

Yes, but in different (better) words.

Hebrews 5:9.
And being made perfect, he became the author of **eternal salvation** *unto all them that obey him.*

Hebrews 9:12.

Neither by the blood of goats and calves, but by his own blood he entered in once into the holy place, having obtained **eternal redemption** *for us.*

Who is safe that isn't secure?

Safe: Secure from liability to harm, injury, danger, or risk: a safe place.

Secure: Sure; certain; assured: secure of victory; secure in religious belief.

Who is redeemed that isn't secure?

Redemption: deliverance from sin; salvation.

So now take these two verses and swap a few words and you have a basis for eternal security in scripture.

Hebrews 5:9.

And being made perfect, he became the author of **_eternal security_** *unto all them that obey him.*

Hebrews 9:12.

Neither by the blood of goats and calves, but by his own blood he entered in once into the holy place, having obtained **_eternal security_** *for us.*

This is a point that is better served without making the point. "Redemption" and "salvation" to me sound much more powerful than the word "security". So I prefer to let scripture read the way it originally intended to read.

The Bible also teaches that if we are saved then we get eternal life. That sounds better than eternal security, and furthermore proves eternal security. The words: "eternal security," aren't in the Bible because they are lexically frail compared to their superlatives.

John 3:15.
That whosoever believeth in him should not perish, but have **_eternal life_**.

Would it matter if it didn't say?

That whosoever believeth in him should not perish but have eternal security.

"Eternal life" sounds so much better than eternal security yet; eternal security is proven by this verse. The doctrine of eternal security is <u>IMPOSSIBLE</u> to refute! There is NO way to controvert it without making scripture read wrongly or contradict itself!

Here are some more scriptures that back up this doctrine.

Luke 10:25.
*And, behold, a certain lawyer stood up, and tempted him, saying, Master, what shall I do to inherit **<u>eternal life</u>**?*

John 6:54.
*Whoso eateth my flesh, and drinketh my blood, hath **<u>eternal life</u>**; and I **<u>will raise him</u>** up at the last day.*

John 10:28.

*And I give unto them **<u>eternal life</u>**; and they shall never perish, neither shall any man pluck them out of my hand.*

James 1:17.

Every good gift and every perfect gift is from above, and cometh down from the Father of lights, with whom is no variableness, neither shadow of turning.

Let's again look at eternal life as a gift from God as this scripture clearly indicates. If you could lose it, it wouldn't be a good gift. When God gave us Jesus, He gave us the greatest gift in the universe. It has descended from heaven to earth 2000 years ago. To lose our salvation, we would have to get into our time machines, go back in time and stop the crucifixion, thus catapulting Jesus back into the firmament.

That would be the only way to give salvation back to God and furthermore lose it!

To <u>not</u> embrace eternal security is absolutely ridiculous!

There's a lot of jive out there about losing your salvation.

Ask someone … anyone, what it would take to lose it.

They may respond with:

Falling into sin.

Unbelief.

Backsliding.

Renouncing God.

Walking away from God or from the faith.

Suicide.

These are all interesting ideas but nevertheless absurd.

If a person could lose his or her salvation in any capacity, everyone would have lost it three minutes after being saved. Because if you could lose your salvation—it would only take one slipup to do so. For a God who demands perfection and then says that Christ is the only one that can make us perfect, all it would take to be imperfect is to break one minor law.

James 2:10, proves this.

For whosoever shall keep the whole law, and yet offend in one point, he is guilty of all.

For us to lose this imputed state of perfection is to say that Christ sinned. If our sins could negate our "righteous standing" with God is to say one of two things. Either we weren't declared perfect in the sight of God by and through Christ or that Christ wasn't righteous at all because of some possible salvific negation on our behalf. Both of which are ludicrous, unbiblical and a slap in God's face.

The doctrine of eternal security is so important that denying it is calling God a liar and a loser! A good Shepherd doesn't lose his sheep, nor does he let them lose their salvation! Such a Shepherd that would forsake his sheep or let them forsake him would be considered a failure! Scripture supports this.

Deuteronomy 31:6.

Be strong and of a good courage, fear not, nor be afraid of them: for the LORD thy God, he it is that doth go with thee; he will not <u>fail</u> thee, nor <u>forsake</u> thee.

If eternal security weren't true then we should just shoot everyone after baptism to ensure that they won't become lost again! Sounds harsh, but oh how true that would be if eternal security weren't true. We must never forget that salvation is something God does for us. And Scripture asserts that what God does, nothing can undo.

Ecclesiastes 3:14.

I know that, whatsoever God doeth, it shall be for ever: nothing can be put to it, nor any thing taken from it: and God doeth it, that men should fear before him.

God bless.

15.License To Sin.

Denying such a doctrine as Sola Fide gives man a license to sin.

"You can't know for certain that you are saved. Sola Fide means that man can just get saved, live anyway that he jolly well pleases and still make it to heaven."

How many times have you heard such nonsense?

Well my counterclaim is this. If you deny Sola Fide, you're denying that Christ's shed blood at Calvary truly saves a person. Otherwise, you have to do something extra to be saved. Works for instance. The biblical accounts of Sola Fide denials would necessarily cause a reversion back to animal sacrifices and circumcisions. We, as modernists, haven't quite made up our minds as to what kind of works must be added to grace, yet we add them anyway.

"Being good," "praying," "confession," "doing penance," "dressing a certain way," "forsaking sin" … whatever.

If these things, accompanied to grace, can save you then why not just allot a designated time to perform them? Once a week, twice a week, once a month—once a year depending on how carnal you are. Obviously, we can sin all we want and then perform such works to atone for our own sins because the permanent atonement Christ offered unto us wasn't enough. This is mere sarcasm to the SolaFidist, but a perilous reality to the Works Salvationist.

Let me clue you in on a little secret. Even in the Bible, the worksists (my coinage for the sake of not falling into the category of anti-Semitic and hyper-Zionistic) preferred works over grace, because they wanted to keep sinning, thus having their sins atoned for. Worksists want to work to cover up their sins. So obviously they wanted to keep sinning.

See how absurd this mentality is.

Now I've heard modern day Conditional Salvationists claim that you can lose your salvation and then get it back through repentance. One extremist even said that that was the case of Peter after each denial. They claim that if Peter had died between his denials that he would've gone to hell. This is specious, unbiblical and ridiculous!

If what this extreme Conditional Salvationists is saying is true, then he's given the world the most convenient license to sin ever! Get saved first thing in the morning, sin inexorably until evenfall, repent before bedtime and batta-bing, you're resaved.

Repeat the process daily.

Get drunk, get buzzed, get sexed, cuss like a Marine, steal, plunder, rape and kill, then return to your abode and say a pithy, ritualistic prayer, sweep the floor and tell God that you're sorry.

The next morning, repeat the process!

Get saved!

Unsaved!

Resaved!

Re-unsaved.

Re-resaved!

Re-re-unsaved!

Re-re-resaved!

Re-re-re-unsaved!

Re-re-re-resaved!

Re-re-re-re-unsaved.

Re-re-re-re-resaved!

Re-re-re-re-re-unsaved!

Re-re-re-re-re-resaved!

Over and over again!

This is ridiculous. I call this Russian roulette theology. Or Hamartiological Calculator theology.

Why because at the end of your salvifically-fluctuant so-called Christian life, that's exactly what you would need … a calculator. And who would be able to determine if you had gotten resaved enough times to weigh against the junctures of unsavedness? Or what if you died during one of your unsaved moments?

Sounds like an even more dangerous "license to sin" than the Once Saved Always Saved version, doesn't it!

Denying Sola Fide is heresy and a qualifier for being a false teacher.

Galatians 1:6-7.

I marvel that ye are so soon removed from him that called you into the grace of Christ unto another gospel: Which is not another; but there be some that trouble you, and would pervert the gospel of Christ.

The Bible warns us that we are not to become false teachers ourselves. Yes, even true Christians can become false teachers.

Galatians 1:8-9.

But though we, or an angel from heaven, preach any other gospel unto you than that which we have preached unto you, let him be accursed. As we said before, so say I now again, if any man preach any other gospel unto you than that ye have received, let him be accursed.

The second epistle of John instructs us on how we are to deal with false teachers.

2 John 10-11.

If there come any unto you, and bring not this doctrine, receive him not into your house, neither bid him God speed: For he that biddeth him God speed is partaker of his evil deeds.

God bless.

16.Lord, Liar or Lunatic?

1 Peter 3:15.

But sanctify the Lord God in your hearts: and be ready always to give an answer to every man that asketh you a reason of the hope that is in you with meekness and fear:

As consummate, professional and lay theologians alike, we all should have by now seen this triple-L slogan. The question is one common in the study of Christian apologetics.

The whole premise is … which one was Jesus?

Lord?

A **Li**ar?

Or a **L**unatic?

He's either the true Son of God or a lying lunatic for claiming to be. As Christians we believe Him to be the true Son of God … Lord and Savior.

This book is a book of apologetics, just not theistic apologetics. I'm not defending the faith against antitheistic worldviews, like atheism, agnosticism and or secular humanism. I'm defending the doctrine of Sola Fide.

And I use the triple-L question as my basis.

Think about it, if the doctrine of Sola Fide isn't true, then Jesus is a liar.

The OSFs have declared him to be a liar.

The OSFs must believe in the possible eternal loss of the believer for it is the backbone of their warped theology. Think about this...

I'm going to address those who think that salvation is by faith and works.

Take this book's theme verse.

John 6:47.

Verily, verily, I say unto you, He that believeth on me hath everlasting life.

Okay, if you don't have a red-letter Bible, go get one! Because those words are the words of Jesus — Himself.

Now humor the idea of faith-plus-works or even losing salvation. If salvation were by faith-plus-works then why isn't it mentioned in John 6:47? If everlasting life could at anytime stop, because of loss, forfeiture or NO WORKS, it thereby fails to be everlasting life. Not only are we contradicting scripture; we are calling Jesus a LIAR! That's as close to committing the unpardonable sin as I personally think someone can do!

Let's not go there.

Matthew 12:31.

Wherefore I say unto you, All manner of sin and blasphemy shall be forgiven unto men: but the blasphemy against the Holy Ghost shall not be forgiven unto men.

Calling Jesus a liar is tantamount to unbelief!

1 John 5:10.

He that believeth on the Son of God hath the witness in himself: he that believeth not God hath <u>made him a liar;</u> because he believeth not the record that God gave of his Son.

You either believe that salvation is by faith alone or you do not. The OSFs don't believe this; hence they call Jesus a liar.

Jesus didn't say: "It is finished … when you obey me or when you work hard or as long as you don't forfeit your faith by and by."

No!

He said it is finished. Period!

He finished our salvation before we had a chance to sin or actuate any kind of good works. Christ didn't finish something so that man could rescind such a divine finality with some departure of faith! To say so or even to think so sacrilegiously calls Jesus a liar!

I don't know about you but I'd rather not call Jesus a liar because it would confirm a position of unbelief as not being my true Savior. Deniers of Sola Fide are doing this either cognizantly or inadvertently, but nonetheless they are doing it!

Jesus is either Lord, Liar or Lunatic. He can't be

all three or any two.

I'm a Solafidian and am here proclaiming Him to be <u>Lord!</u>

2 Peter 3:18.

But grow in grace, and in the knowledge of our Lord and Savior Jesus Christ. To him be glory both now and for ever. Amen.

The OSF is not only calling God a liar; he is also metamorphosing Christian faith into polytheism. Think about it ... to deny Sola Fide is to add works.

Jesus plus works.

Jesus plus rituals.

Jesus plus speaking in tongues.

Jesus plus righteous living.

Jesus plus confession.

These "pluses" could easily be supplanted for...

Jesus plus Buddha.

Jesus plus Quezacoatal.

Jesus plus Brahman.

Jesus plus Zeus.

Jesus plus Satan.

That's polytheism and so is denying Sola Fide!

God bless.

17.Christ Alone.

My defense for those that deny Sola Fide, but are sincere in their love for Christ. Although, undoubtedly, there are so-called Christians out there, that are <u>lost</u> and don't love the <u>true</u> Christ at all that deny the doctrine of Sola Fide, fortunately not every OSF is that way. Caveat.***Keep in mind this chapter was written several years ago. My doctrinal opinion has changed on some topics since.***

Well how do we know who is who?

Some people have never trusted in Christ. They've only trusted in religion in order to be saved, which inevitably, leads to a works-plus doctrinal mentality. Others have sincerely trusted in Christ, but thereafter, and out of ignorance, bad preaching or misinterpretation of scripture, have relegated that trust to: "Christ-plus-something-else."

Honestly. Only God knows who is really saved.

So many people malign Catholicism. They say that Catholics aren't really saved because they are trusting in works or sacraments to save them. But as far as I've observed and what I've resourcefully scrutinized by historical studies on the Catholic Saints, most Catholics do believe in and love Jesus

Christ. So I must conclude that they are veraciously trusting in Christ—but alas some may be ignorantly adding works.

The bottom line is if you trust Christ for salvation, you are saved. It is Christ alone that saves, so if you trust Christ, despite whether or not you add works, your trust in Christ is saving you ALONE! The works outside of this trust become baggage and self-oriented.

As far as Catholicism is concerned, if they or any other religious sect, including cultic religions, I.e., Jehovah's Witness, LDS, Unitarian Universalists, trust in Christ, they are saved. The problem with these cultic religions is that they've changed who Christ is. And so have the OSFs. I don't think that God will hold such ignorance against them if they have sincerely sought God. Scriptures say that if you believe in Jesus you are saved. It doesn't say that you have to know everything about Jesus in order to be saved. If you belong to one of these factions and trust Christ to be saved, He will save you even if your trust is not in His "aloneness." His aloneness is not perpetuated by your trust in the aloneness, just your trust in Christ.

If you add works or ancillary rituals, such secondary acts; you are simply stymieing your assurance of salvation, for they are just wasteful gestures on your part—with no salvific bearing whatsoever!

But wait a minute; hasn't my attitude toward

the OSFs thus far suggested that most are not saved? I feel that there are certain people that don't want others to be saved — so they institute impossible standards to deter others from coming to Christ. These people obviously don't love others. Unless everyone is selfsame to Adolph Hitler, we shouldn't wish hell upon anyone. I've met people from The Church Of Christ that overtly didn't want sinners go to heaven and preached sermon after sermon on this point as if the entire message of the gospel was: forsake your sin, period!

Those, I fear may still be lost!

Back to Christ alone.

After trusting Christ alone, works will be exchanged for eternal rewards.

So yes, Catholics who sincerely love Christ are SAVED! Same with any other sincere works-based denominations. If you want my opinion, 99 percent out of all the Christians I've ever met, Protestant and Catholic alike have added works to salvation in some manner and many don't even realize it. Calvinists have added works in saying that if you are really saved then you will evidence your salvation by works. That's the same as adding works. Even most OSAS Baptists have suggested that works evidence your salvation. That's no different then saying that you must work for your salvation. Because it is saying that you must produce evidence of your salvation by works, which requires works to obtain such evidence. It's all just a big game of semantic wordplay.

It's Christ alone that saves!

If you are placing trust in Christ plus works, it doesn't necessarily mean that you aren't saved; it could mean that you are in fact saved with a misplaced trust in something else that can't save you! Such a person could have at one point in time trusted in Christ alone. The people I'm worried about are those who have never trusted in Christ alone and have always added works to the gospel. God doesn't expect much faith, just faith. Look at this verse:

Matthew 17:20.
And Jesus said unto them, Because of your unbelief: for verily I say unto you, If ye have faith as a grain of mustard seed, ye shall say unto this mountain, Remove hence to yonder place; and it shall remove; and nothing shall be impossible unto you.

God bless.

18.Christians Aren't Sinless, But They Do Sin Less!

Discussed.

Psalm 40:12.
For troubles without number surround me; my sins have overtaken me, and I cannot see. They are more than the hairs of my head, and my heart fails within me.

Ephesians 4:22. (NKJV)

That you put off, concerning your former conduct, the old man which <u>grows</u> corrupt according to the deceitful lusts.

This truth needs to be stated. So many times, I hear Christians say that they are not *sinless*, but they do *sin less*. Is this true or false? The following thesis proves this to be false.

First of all, to say that we sin less than: "unbelievers" or "our old self" is to misunderstand just how much we sin. The Bible states that Job had to ask God how much he sinned for he didn't even know.

Job 13:23.

How many are mine iniquities and sins? make me to know my transgression and my sin.

Saying that we *sin less* is a mismeasurement and an underestimation whereupon questioning God how much iniquity we have would be null and void. In such a case why would Job have done so?

Take a look at this verse.

Hebrews 9:28.
So Christ was once offered to bear the sins of <u>many</u>; and unto them that look for him shall he appear the second time without sin unto salvation.

Some people say that this means that Christ died for the sins of many people. However, we know that Christ died not only for many but also for all people! To support the popular understanding of this verse is to postulate an extreme Calvinistic viewpoint, which is highly refutable. Then there are those who say that the ones who don't accept Christ are referring to the *minority* — antithetical to the — *the many*.

This is also not true. Christ died for everyone's sin, even the lost that will end up in hell. (1 John 2:2.) The only sin that can send a sinner to hell is not believing in Christ. This scripture as it has been revealed to me is referring to the fact that Christ died for our sins and they are MANY!

John 3:16.

For God so loved the world, that he gave his only

begotten Son, that whosoever believeth in him should not perish, but have everlasting life.

The world means everyone in the world.

"Many" according to the dictionary is:

(Constituting or forming a large number; numerous: multitudinous, an uncountable amount of something.)

So the Bible says that we sin uncountably.

I've heard Christians say that they can go several days without sinning. What I should've responded to this nonsense with was.

"Well if you are trying to get into the Guinness Book of World Records, you just blew it with that mendacious statement."

1 Timothy 1:15.

This is a faithful saying, and worthy of all acceptation, that Christ Jesus came into the world to save sinners; of whom I am chief.

Paul considered himself a chief sinner. Synonymous phrases could be "Top sinner," "king sinner," or "paramount sinner." If a person maintains that they can go several days without sinning they are elevating themselves above the apostle Paul, which is arrogantly preposterous!

Scripture also says that Paul was not only an apostle but also a preacher and a teacher.

2 Timothy 1:11.

Whereunto I am appointed a preacher, and an apostle, and a teacher of the Gentiles.

If you can go a few days without sinning, then you must have a greater credential status than the apostle Paul who was a threefold servant and champion of God. Self-righteousness is the only thing that ensues from thinking that you don't sin all the time and it is underpinned by pure hamartiological ignorance.

Take a look at this grid.

****

Sin. Sin. Sin. Sin. Sin. Sin. Sin. Sin. Sin. Sin. Sin. Sin. Sin. Sin. Sin. Sin. Sin. Sin. Sin. Sin. Sin. Sin. Sin. Sin. Sin. Sin. Sin. Sin. Sin. Sin. Sin. Sin. Sin. Sin. Sin. Sin. Sin. Sin. Sin. Sin. Sin. Sin. Sin. Sin. Sin. Sin. Sin. Sin. Sin. Sin. Sin. Sin. Sin. Sin. Sin. Sin. Sin. Sin. Sin. Sin. Sin. Sin. Sin. Sin. Sin. Sin. Sin. Sin. Sin. Sin. Sin. Sin. Sin. Sin. Sin. Sin. Sin. Sin. Sin. Sin. Sin. Sin. Sin. Sin. Sin. Sin. Sin. Sin. Sin. Sin. Sin. Sin. Sin. Sin. Sin. Sin. Sin.

If you didn't sin all the time, then the grid would look like this.

Sin. Sin. Sin. Sin. Self-righteousness. Sin. Sin. Sin. Self-righteousness. Sin. Sin. Self-righteousness Sin. Sin. Sin. Sin. Sin. Self-righteousness. Self-righteousness. Sin. Self-righteousness. Self-righteousness. Self-righteousness. Self-righteousness. Sin. Sin. Self-righteousness. Sin. Sin. Sin. Sin. Self-righteousness Sin. Sin. Sin. Sin. Sin. Sin. Sin. Sin. Sin. Sin. Self-righteousness. Self-righteousness. Self-righteousness. Sin. Sin. Sin. Sin. Sin. Sin. Sin. Sin.

See, when you're not sinning you are being self-righteous. And that's a sin. Some may object and say that I'm not giving a Christian any allowance to be Christlike. That's not what I'm doing. I'm saying that anyone who says they don't sin is practicing self-righteousness as the above display illustrates. True holiness manufactured by Christ alone through us wouldn't brag on itself.

And if it did, it would have transmogrified into smelly, itchy, rotten-to-the-core filthy self-righteousness! And we don't want to go there.

****

Job 35:2.
Thinkest thou this to be right, that thou saidst, My righteousness is more than God's?

Our self-righteousness presumptively trumps

God's and is an affront to His holy nature. The instant we cross over into the self-righteous zone, we've rendered God's true righteousness and holiness into something less than our own filthy-rags righteousness. Ouch! When we become self-righteous, we are at the same level as the wicked Pharisees.

Matthew 13, verse 23 calls the "self-righteous" or Pharisees hypocrites.

But woe unto you, scribes and Pharisees, hypocrites! for ye shut up the kingdom of heaven against men: for ye neither go in yourselves, neither suffer ye them that are entering to go in.

Matthew 23, verse 24 says that they will be susceptible to a greater damnation.

Woe unto you, scribes and Pharisees, hypocrites! for ye devour widows' houses, and for a pretence make long prayer: therefore ye shall receive the greater damnation.

The Pharisees were in sin denial.

1 John 1:10.

If we say that we have not sinned, we make him a liar, and his word is not in us.

Look at the statement: *"I can go a few days without sinning."*

Let's add something with correlation to the meaning of this verse. Keep in mind; I'm not trying to add to the scripture.

Revelation 22:18.

For I testify unto every man that heareth the words of the prophecy of this book, If any man shall add unto these things, God shall add unto him the plagues that are written in this book.

This is not an appendage to scripture; it is a clarifying addition to the connotation of scripture.

Take a look at the new rendering of 1 John 1:10.

If we say that we have not sinned (<u>in a few days or that much</u>), *we make him a liar, and his word is not in us.*

The deniers of daily sinning are in a deceptive La-La-land.

Deuteronomy 11:16.

Take heed to yourselves, that your heart be not deceived, and ye turn aside, and serve other gods, and worship them.

When we think we don't sin all the time, we are deceived and the gods we serve are self-righteousness and human morality, not God! That was the crux of Pharisaism. They brandished their phylacteries, which was an insult to the scriptures thereon.

Revelation 12:10.

And I heard a loud voice saying in heaven, Now is come salvation, and strength, and the kingdom of our God, and the power of his Christ: for the accuser of our brethren is cast down, which accused them before our God <u>day and</u>

night.

According to the concordance this is talking about Satan accusing us all day and all nightlong. In order to be able to do so, we must sin quite often. If we didn't sin so much this scripture could say that Satan accuses us every once in a while. But instead it says: "day and night." That's as durative as it gets. If we weren't sinning so often, then Satan wouldn't be able to accuse us at all, let alone so profusely.

The idea is not to laud continual sin; the idea is to admit to it. When we come to Christ, we come to Him defeated.

Matthew 11:28.

Come unto me, all ye that labour and are heavy laden, and I will give you rest.

When you come to Christ defeated and heavy laden, it is not because of little, infrequent and pithy sins. It is because of burdensome, ponderous, continuous and besetting sins!

Some say it may not have to do with sins at all. If it weren't sins, then Christ would not be the proper entity to come to. You could go to your local doctor or therapist. The reason to go to Christ is because of sin. The heavy-ladenness is a result of sin. If we didn't have sin in the world, it would be utopian and winsome all the time.

That's not reality.

The Bible tells us to pray without ceasing.

1 Thessalonians 5:17.

Pray without ceasing.

If we didn't sin that much such an exhortation in terms of sin wouldn't be necessary or even in the Bible.

We must constantly be on guard!

Because we sin so much!

Many will read this and claim that I'm attacking righteousnesses. I'm not. I'm only attacking self-righteousness. Righteousness is commendable and for the sake of the believer's rewards in heaven.

2 Samuel 22:21.

The LORD <u>rewarded</u> me according to my <u>righteousness</u>: according to the cleanness of my hands hath he recompensed me.

This whole "sin less theory" doesn't fly very well because look at how Satan influences us.

Here's what Satan does to the unbeliever.

He blinds them. 2 Corinthians 4:4.

He uses them. Acts 13:8-10.

He snatches them. Luke 8:12.

Here's what Satan does to the believer.

He hinders them. 1 Thessalonians 2:18.

He accuses them. Revelation 12:10.

He assaults them. Ephesians 6:10-12.

He deceives them. Matthew 13:38-39.

He tempts them. Genesis 3:1-5.

He influences them. Matthew 18:21-23.

He oppresses them. Job 15:20.

Christians aren't *sinless* but they do *sin less* is utter nonsense!

We've all heard this and some of us have actually said it but to honestly believe this is to misunderstand what a Christian conception of sin should be. Christians sin more than non-Christians only because the law has added so many more sins. It's not that the nature of a Christian's sin is that of the non-Christian, nor should their attitude about sin be one and the same as the non-believer. It is however the law that gives Christians more ways and opportunities to sin.

Think about it.

What does a non-Christian have to do to be a thief?

They have to commit larceny, become a

pickpocket or shoplift.

Now, what does a Christian have to do to be a thief?

They must simply neglect to tithe. (Malachi 3:8.)

Christians sin more because the law has opened their eyes to the full gamut of sinfulness, not because they literally do more heinous things than a non-believer. God forbid! A Christian that thinks they sin less than a non-Christian is ignorant of the law.

Romans 3:20.

Therefore by the deeds of the law no flesh will be justified in His sight, for by the law is the knowledge of sin.

Another example would be the idea that a non-Christian has a list of sins. 10 to be exact. He fails 9 out of the 10 on the list. But a Christian, as diligent as he may be, fails fifty of the ones on his list. So, who's the bigger sinner?

The Christian, right?

Yup.

But only because the Christian's list was so much greater!

The idea here is sin awareness!

As Christians, we are not under the law so such a failure has nothing to do with our salvation. The non-Christian is in peril because the only sin that will send a person to hell is unbelief in Christ! John 8:24.

God bless.

19.Fruitless Christians.

The idea of Sola Fide bothers so many Christians because it seems that the concept of *faith alone* annuls the fact that we need to bear fruit as growing believers. In others words, we can possess the Holy Spirit, but not walk in the Spirit. To the shock of some of you, this Solafidian strongly believes we need to walk in the Spirit to the best of our ability. But no specified amount of fruit bearing is mentioned in the Bible as to how much fruition one would need to achieve in order to be saved. This is the one reason that the doctrine of Sola Fide is infallible. Because it does give a specific means as to how one can be saved and know that he or she is saved!

Faith alone!

But don't get me wrong, bearing fruit is what God desires and is crucial for enjoying your salvation.

There are tons of people that will tell you that if you are saved, you will automatically walk in the spirit. And as Christians, we definitely should! But it's not a mandate, nor is it automatic. It is something that we must choose to allow God to do through us. (Colossians 1:29.)

So, yes there are some Christians that bear what seems like no fruit at all!

This is the one subset where the OSFs and I are

in agreement.

However, I will not make this an issue of salvation. If I could scare the hellfire out of someone who bears no fruit, I would. But from experience, I know that fire-and-brimstoning just doesn't work. You may scare someone for a few minutes into saying a terse prayer but after that verbal assertion is seemingly made, they will go right back out into their void of sinful, meaningless triviality.

The best way to lead someone to Christ or even to Christian discipleship is by and through love. Love is what motivates us to serve Christ and bear fruit. Not fear, duty, or reluctant obligation. If you really love God and can just get an infinitesimal foretaste of how much He loves you, you won't want to sit in front of the Boob-tube for twelve hours a day watching a bunch of celluloid trash — at least you shouldn't!

I'm not talking about gripping sins or addictions here. Because Satan engineers most of that. I'm talking about the one sin Satan, although responsible for, doesn't foment on the basis of our spiritual neutralization.

That's right. Satan lets many Christians remain spiritually neutral so that they won't come to humility and thereupon obedience. Because obedience would bring forth spiritual growth! And Satan doesn't want that at all.

Back to my thesis.

Ephesians 4:30.

And grieve not the holy Spirit of God, whereby ye are sealed unto the day of redemption.

The idea that we can grieve the spirit suggests that some people will grieve it for quite lengthy durations, like between Sundays after-church to the time they recite their once-a-week, perfunctory, bedtime prayer.

It's really quite sad but if everyone who was saved automatically walked in the spirit, we'd all bear perhaps a prefigured, set amount of fruit. But sadly, there are Christians out there that bear no visible, evidential fruit at all. That perfunctory prayer they say once a week if their memory is acute enough to remind them is between them and God and unseen to anyone else.

Scripture measures the fruit of a believer in this manner.

Thirtyfold. Sixtyfold. Hundredfold.
Matthew 13:8.
But other fell into good ground, and brought forth fruit, some an hundredfold, some sixtyfold, some thirtyfold.

This seems to contradict the idea of bearing none or little to no fruit, but I'd have to say that, in some cases, the thirtyfolders are those that only bear fruit privately.

If the Holy Spirit automatically bears fruit upon a believer's salvation, I have to deem that it would opt to bear <u>hundredfold</u> fruit all the time. But unfortunately it doesn't until and unless spiritual maturation is being sought on a daily basis.

Galatians 5:25.
If we live in the Spirit, let us also walk in the Spirit.

Some people say that this proves that those who are saved will inevitably walk in the spirit.

It is not saying that at all.

It is referring to Christians who live in the spirit, but this is a hortatory verse, not a declarative. It exhorts us who live in the spirit to also walk in the Spirit. It is not saying that we absolutely will. It is saying that we should. The "absolutely will theory" negates our freewill.

For this verse to suggest that a Christian will automatically bear fruit; it would have to read:

If we live in the Spirit, <u>we will certainly</u> walk in the Spirit.

The *let us also* is an encouragement for us to walk in the Spirit, it doesn't — sad to say — guarantee that we will.

Another hortatory verse is.

Galatians 5:16.
This I say then, Walk in the Spirit, and ye shall not fulfil the lust of the flesh.

So how do we know if someone is saved based

on this hermeneutical premise? Aren't I allowing everyone who professes to be saved, those of which that act worse than Howard Stern, bearing less fruit than a withered tree in a barren tundra, the right to think that they will end up in heaven all because of a single act of faith?

And that is a good question considering this book is themed, "faith alone," *Sola Fide.*

The answer is that a fruitless Christian will be chronically unhappy. Not should be, ... but ... WILL BE!

No doubt, God chastises His children. (Hebrews 12:8-11.) That chastisement is to get us to bear fruit. If a professing Christian, albeit fruitless, lives a Chitty-chitty-bang-bang, happy-go-lucky, Pollyannaish life without chastisement for the course of many years, then something is dead wrong!

The Bible is clear that sin causes sorrow.

Psalm 51:12.
Restore unto me the joy of thy salvation; and uphold me with thy free spirit.

This is not someone asking for his salvation back, as clearly we both should know by now that salvation cannot be lost in any capacity. This is for a backslider, a fruitless Christian who is miserable, because of chastisement. David wanted his JOY back. If you deliberately sin, even once, it can sap the joy you have with God away in the blink of an eye!

Fruit-bearing is what grants us joy. (Galatians 5:22.)

But chastisement, due to fruitlessness is very grievous.

Hebrews 12:11.
Now no chastening for the present seemeth to be joyous, but <u>grievous</u>: nevertheless afterward it yieldeth the peaceable fruit of righteousness unto them which are exercised thereby.

The sine qua non, is this...

Fruitlessness and worldly happiness don't mix!

Fruitlessness and misery is reality.

Frui<u>tful</u>ness and joy is PERFECT and biblical!

If you are bearing no fruit and finish reading this subset and then nonchalantly go back to your business, with a devil-may-care attitude, as if you had just read a trivial excerpt from the newspaper, God will bring castigatory tragedy your way!

Luke 13:9.
And if it bear fruit, well: and if not, then after that thou shalt <u>cut it down</u>.

If you finish reading this and are inspired to bear fruit, my encouragement is to read your Bible so that God will instead bless you.

John 15:8.
Herein is my Father glorified, that ye bear much fruit;

so shall ye be my disciples.

Psalm 29:11.

The LORD will give strength unto his people; the LORD will bless his people with peace.

God bless.

20.Our Part.

John 3:16.

Seems Too Good To Be True!

This book is pregnant with scads of negative propaganda that permeates the true untainted message of the gospel. Some may even deduce that I just wrote it to address all the OSFs, Works Salvationists, Lordship Salvationists, heretics, fakes, false teachers and Judaizers at large in the Christian world.

And, frankly such falsehoods and the propagators thereof fomented a large part my inspiration and aspiration for writing this book, but aside from that, let me tell you why this book is duly necessary.

Because most of all the Christians that I've conversed with at some point in their life were adding works to their theology and not fully embracing Sola Fide (faith alone).

Even, I myself have much to learn about it. It's extremely difficult to understand the concept of something being absolutely FREE! It is the nature of man to want to defray for all that he receives. Such a defrayal, in reference to salvation, seems to substantiate the reality of the gospel.

But it shouldn't!

Why can't two people just intimately hold each other? Like girlfriend and boyfriend. Works, deeds, and duty make the relationship appear more realistic. The idea of "too good to be true" is universally unfathomable and unaccepted. If we really believe that God is good and are not just spewing out this verbiage as if it were a cheap cliché, then what is wrong with salvation being absolutely FREE?

Nothing!

So many people are implicitly trying to do their part in either earning their salvation, keeping their salvation or proving their salvation. These are the three popular watchwords in any works-salvation doctrine.

I've even heard someone say that:

"God did His part, now you gotta do yours!"

It was uttered with arrogance and vitriol amid a crowded church hallway.

My unvoiced response to him now is:

"Yeah, man does have to do his part but guess what that is. It's to receive salvation. How do we do that? We must simply believe. Sola Fide. Faith alone!"

Take a look at:

John 3:16.
For God so loved the world, that he gave his only

begotten Son, that whosoever believeth in him should not perish, but have everlasting life.

Now let's exegetically break this verse apart.
***For God so loved the world — (God's part).

***That he gave his only begotten Son — (God's part).

***That whosoever <u>believeth</u> in him — (Our part).

***Should not perish — (God's first promise).

***But have everlasting life — (God's second promise).

***It doesn't get any simpler than this.

Man's part is to simply believe. Arguing this is a patent expression of unbelief. So the next time someone says that: *you gotta do your part.* Ask them what they mean. If they say anything other than "faith alone," their own belief is in question.

Some may protest that believing means something other than just "believing the facts." "Believeth" in Greek is *Pisteuo,* which means to be persuaded or to trust. Some Arminians try to back up their heretical theology by saying that Christians have to do more than just believe and that they must live a committed life unto Christ unwaveringly.

Some say that belief must be actualized by a commitment of works in order to be true belief.

But that speculation has too many loose ends and nobody can be certain that they are committed enough. When we put faith in Christ, we have committed unto Him. Those that try to live robotically committed lives have not committed unto Christ at all. If commitment were not faith alone than it would entail works.

Romans 4:5 refutes that.

But to him that worketh not, but believeth on him that justifieth the ungodly, his faith is counted for righteousness.

This scripture does an apt job in severing "belief" from "committed works."

Believing in Christ alone through faith alone that His finished work on the cross is what saves puts us in the same category as Abraham. He was persuaded that he was saved and eternally secure.

Romans 4:21-22.
And being fully <u>persuaded</u> that, what he had promised, he was able also to perform. And therefore it was imputed to him for righteousness.

The latter part of verse 22 (all-capitalized) is referencing to the Abrahamic covenant found in Genesis 15:6.

Salvation in the OT and NT has never changed. (Isaiah 45:22.)

And it is being persuaded that Christ will save

you. That comes only by faith alone.

John 3:16 is the entire gospel, but it doesn't replace the other Sola Fide verses as being equally significant. We need to watch out for those that try to change the meaning of verses even as simple as this popular one. The gospel is only good news when it is not misrepresented.

The word "Gospel" in Greek, *Euaggelion,* literally means: "Good message."

If Sola Fide isn't the good message, I don't know what is! It's funny how man loves to be ergophobic (hater of work) when it comes to industrial or factorial labors but in terms of working for salvation, man is ironically slavishly masochistic.

God bless.

21. The Doctrine of Original Sin.

Ecclesiastes 7:20.
For there is not a just man upon earth, that doeth good, and sinneth not.

So many Christians are deluded and look at their own post-salvation sin experience as not being "that bad" or "that big of a deal." I hear a lot of pat phrases that go something like the following:

I no longer practice sin.

I don't habitually sin.

Christians are no longer slaves to sin.

I sin but not that much or not as much as others.

Man wasn't born in original sin.

The Bible speaks against this.

John 8:34.
Jesus answered them, Verily, verily, I say unto you, Whosoever committeth sin is the servant (slave) of sin.

"Committeth" in Greek is: *Poieo*. Which simply means to <u>perform</u> or <u>do</u>.

There are ridiculous rumors out there that the

word *committeth* means a "continual practice of." The concordance does not specify this at all. It simply says: to do, to work, to shew. Jesus is saying that anyone who commits sins, that includes us — the saved — is a slave to sin. And we will remain a slave to sin until we repent and confess. (1 John 1:9.)

Here's what sin really is in the Christian life.

<u>Sin</u> is simply a slow, continual, recurrent act of physical suicide.

<u>Sin</u> is a demand for heaven or heavenly pleasures, NOW!

<u>Sin</u>, *hamartia*, missing the mark.

<u>Sin</u> is simply taking your mind off God.

<u>Sin</u> is the biggest rip off in the world.

<u>Sin</u> is the biggest paradox. (For we know how regrettable it is but we do it anyway.)

<u>Sin</u> is something we do everyday whether we realize it or not!

<u>Sin</u> is a genetic condition we are stuck with!

To disagree with any of the antecedent statements is to misunderstand the biblical understanding of sin.

Too often, to much dismay, I hear people talk about how a Christian lives or is supposed to live. But in my own experience, what they say is totally bogus.

Scripture is clear that as we grow in Christ, our sin-awareness radar illumines brighter and brighter everyday.

Romans 3:20. (NIRV).

So it can't be said that anyone will be made right with God by obeying the law. Not at all! The law makes us more aware of our sin.

These are Paul's words, not mine. So don't shoot the messenger.

Romans 7:8.

But sin, taking occasion by the commandment, wrought in me all manner of concupiscence. For without the law sin was dead.

In case you are wondering what "concupiscence" means, it is the equivalent to "covetous desires."

What this verse is saying is that the more we understand God's law the more sinful, or covetous we realize we are!

How does one get off saying that he doesn't continue in sin when the law continues to reveal just how depraved and sinful we really are the more we understand it?

We are not supposed to assume how much we sin.

We are supposed to ask God how truly sinful we are.

Look at Job.

Job 13:23.
How many are mine iniquities and sins? make me to know my transgression and my sin.

Notice that Job didn't say, "I don't sin that much." He asked God, wanting to know: *how much, how many, the enormity, extent, and breadth* of his sinfulness.

The reason we shouldn't have an opaque understanding about our own sinfulness is because we are exhorted to confess our sins. You can't confess what you won't own up to.

1 John 1:9.

If we confess our sins, he is faithful and just to forgive us our sins, and to cleanse us from all unrighteousness.

It is very important to confess your sins otherwise man has a tendency to redefine what sin is. I've even heard Christians say that cussing wasn't really a sin. They twisted scriptures out of context in order to support their fallacious point. Why couldn't this cusser just have confessed his sin? It would've been a lot easier than misapplying scripture. Some people don't understand the doctrine of justification, so they have to find ways to makebelieve that they don't sin anymore.

Taken to a crazy extreme, some people will say that they can go an entire day without sinning.

Ridiculous!

Scripture says to confess your faults one to another.

How is this not daily? Do you go a day without interacting with your peers?

James 5:16.
Confess your faults one to another, and pray one for another, that ye may be healed. The effectual fervent prayer of a righteous man availeth much.

What about this verse?

Ezekiel 45:23.
And seven days of the feast he shall prepare a burnt offering to the LORD, seven bullocks and seven rams without blemish daily the seven days; and a kid of the goats daily for a sin offering.

In the Old Testament, if a person didn't sin daily, then why would they need to offer a sin offering daily?

****

Take a look at this allegory.

Let's say that Bad Billy goes out and gets wasted, fornicates, kills three people arbitrarily, breaks into five cars and burglarizes their CD players.

He comes home and beats his wife to a bruised pulp and then cusses vociferously while snorting line-after-line of cocaine. He does this everyday!

He has indeed broken some of God's laws, and in fact a lot of God's laws!

You could say that he's broken virtually all of them. He's even got sins that we don't even know about. Closet sins!

Now, let's say that there's this other guy, Good Gary who goes to church every week, reads his Bible all the time. Doesn't cuss, smoke, chew or hang around with those that do. But every once in a while he exaggerates to his girlfriend on how much he bench-pressed at the gym on the days he works out.

That makes him a liar.

What does the Bible say about liars?

Revelation 21:8.
But the fearful, and unbelieving, and the abominable, and murderers, and whoremongers, and sorcerers, and idolaters, and all (unsaved) <u>liars</u>, shall have their part in the lake which burneth with fire and brimstone: which is the second death.

It also says that everyone lies, without exception.

Romans 3:4.

God forbid: yea, let God be true, <u>but every man a</u>

liar; as it is written, That thou mightest be justified in thy sayings, and mightest overcome when thou art judged.

Psalms 116:11.
I said in my haste, <u>All</u> men are <u>liars</u>.

So, who's guiltier? Bad Billy or Good Gary.

The answer is that they are both equally as guilty!

James 2:10.

For whosoever shall keep the whole law, and yet offend in one point, he is guilty of all.

Good Gary's lie makes him as guilty as the murderous, drug-addicted, foulmouthed Bad Billy!

According to God's law.

The law continually brings to surface just how sinful we are.

The "I don't continue to sin theory" falls flat on its face in light of scripture.

Proverbs 24:16.
For a just man falleth <u>seven times</u>, and riseth up again: but the wicked shall fall into mischief.

The Hebrew word for falleth takes on two meanings:

Naphal, to fall away, to fail or to fall short. Each of which denotes, sin.

Nabel, is the same word and not used in this verse. It is "falleth". This has a different connotation altogether. To wither, to wear away or to literally fall as leaves fall from a tree.

Compare to.

Isaiah 34:4.
And all the host of heaven shall be dissolved, and the heavens shall be rolled together as a scroll: and all their host shall fall down, as the leaf <u>falleth</u> off from the vine, and as a falling fig from the fig tree.

What Proverbs 24:16 is saying is that even just men (Christians) fall short quite often. It says they fall seven times. This could mean a day. This could mean an hour—who knows? But the bottom line is that man falls short quite a lot!

This whole continual practice argument is as substantive as vapor. Because nobody can decide what it means to continue to practice sin. Nobody! Does it mean once a week, twice a day, ten times a year, consistently for three weeks but then you stop for a while? Nobody knows what it means to practice sin. I practice martial arts, but lately I've only practiced for a few hours over a four-month period. But this is still practice.

Some people say that practicing sins means to commit a certain sin everyday. But is it logical to divide sins into subsections? Everyone sins everyday! It may not be the same sin, but it is still sin. For instance. Let's say I cuss on Monday, overeat on

Tuesday, fornicate on Wednesday, cheat on my taxes on Thursday, wax in laziness on Friday, get drunk on Saturday and skip church on Sunday. I've sinned everyday. Doesn't that qualify me as a practicing sinner just as much as someone who commits the same sin on a daily basis?

For a just man falleth <u>seven times</u>, and riseth up again: but the wicked shall fall into mischief.

Imagine someone looking at porn seven times a day or cussing seven times an hour. The idea however is that even though we fall short, we do rise up again and are called back to a renewed fellowship with God. We can debate all day long about how sinful we are either *before* or *after* salvation but the important thing to remember is that Christ died for the ungodly, that's us! Period.

Romans 5:6.
For when we were yet without strength, in due time Christ died for the ungodly.

God bless.

22.Struggling With Sin.

(((("Struggle.")))

(To contend with, to war against, to fight or conflict; the act of physical struggling.)

Romans 7:19.

For the good that I would I do not: but the evil which I would not, that I do.

Galatians 5:12.

For the flesh lusteth against the Spirit, and the Spirit against the flesh: and these are contrary the one to the other: so that ye cannot do the things that ye would.

****

Every Christian alive possessing a human anatomy struggles with sin!

PERIOD!

Little sins.

Big sins.

Perpetual sins.

Mortal sins.

Venial sins.

Slipups.

Addictions.

Carnal thoughts.

Take your pick.

As Christians, we struggle with sin. If a person claims to not struggle with sin then he is either not saved, in a cult that has redefined what sin is or just plain-out steeped in demonic deception. Read what the Bible says about non-believers.

Psalm 14:3.

They are all gone aside, they are all together become filthy: there is none that doeth good, no, not one.

It's clear that no one pleases God without God's help.

But in this subset we are dealing with the "struggle of sin." Only a true believer can claim to struggle with sin. Non-believers don't have this struggle. They sin without any qualms, scruples or pangs of post-sin guilt.

Christians know they struggle with sin because they openly acknowledge their sins.

Psalm 38:3-4.

There is no soundness in my flesh because of thine anger; neither is there any rest in my bones because of my sin. For mine iniquities are gone over mine head: as an heavy burden they are too heavy for me.

A professor of sin in NT times, like in the latter verse must have the Holy Spirit in them; otherwise no such profession could be made. Now I know some non-Christians may use the word sin, but they do it jestingly and in some occasions as an apothegmatic slang. I've even heard Macgyver, who plays the role of a moralistic agnostic, use the phrase: "the wages of sin." It just happened to be germane to the Catholic theme of that episode.

But non-Christians typically won't use the word "sins" as a contrite expression to import a Biblical conception of man's intrinsically evil nature.

Read on.

Psalm 51:3-4.

For I acknowledge my transgressions: and my sin is ever before me.

Not only was David acknowledging the lascivious sin he committed with Bathsheba to the prophet Nathan, but he was also copious in expressing just how extortionately rotten his sin was in the eyes of God.

Non-Christians haven't come to their senses insofar that they even feel a need to confess, repent, and get saved. In fact, they couldn't care less!

Proverbs 30:20.

Such is the way of an adulterous woman; she eateth, and wipeth her mouth, and saith, I have done no wickedness.

Here's another example of a non-Christian that is not concerned about the perilous consequences of sin.

Proverbs 28:22.

He that hasteth to be rich hath an evil eye, and considereth not that poverty shall come upon him.

The consequence to this sin, and in the case of most sin, was poverty.

Psalm 10:4.

The wicked, through the pride of his countenance, will not seek after God: God is not in all his thoughts.

Honestly, is this type of person actually struggling with sin?

No.

God would have to be in his thoughts in order for him to be struggling.

So, now, we've established that the only strugglers of sin are true believers. But what about when we hear people say that we need to forsake our sins. If a street preacher, evangelist, or any other type of person claiming to be spreading the gospel, speaks salvifically or evangelistically about forsaking sins, he is not giving you the true gospel.

The Pauline gospel could be put into these words.

"The Bible says that we are all sinners. Romans 3:23. We have no way to stop sinning. Neither have we any way to make ourselves right with God on our own. Christ died on the cross as a substitutionary atonement for us. The only hope we have in being saved is to come to Him and simply believe in Him. Then we are eternally saved."

If someone says: "You better turn or burn. Forsake your sins and follow Christ," they haven't given you the true gospel. First of all, they've got the order wrong, … backwards! This is not only a <u>false gospel</u>, but is a message bereft of the true gospel altogether.

Forsaking your sin is never a command for unbelievers, for that would be impossible without the assistance of the Holy Spirit. The message to unbelievers is always to put faith in Christ alone for salvation. The directives to forsake sin are always for believers, but are not contingent upon either attaining or sustaining salvation.

1 Peter 2:1. (NLT)

So get rid of all evil behavior. Be done with all deceit, hypocrisy, jealousy, and all unkind speech.

This is referring to newborn Christians.

The epistles were always written to Christians. In this epistle, Peter was warning the outside-of-the-church believers to beware of false teachers. Sin was always a stumbling block in exercising discernment.

Forsaking your sin is not possible without Christ, (John 15:5) so this verse is not a prerequisite for salvation. If you keep reading in the first epistle of Peter, you will discover more hortatory scriptures that encourage the importance for the believer to forsake sin. Not for salvation, but for fellowship.

1 Peter 3:9-11.

Not rendering evil for evil, or railing for railing: but contrariwise blessing; knowing that ye are thereunto called, that ye should inherit a blessing. For he that will love life, and see good days, let him refrain his tongue from evil, and his lips that they speak no guile: Let him eschew evil, and do good; let him seek peace, and ensue it.

Yeah, yeah, yeah, so what! This doesn't prove anything the skeptic might claim.

Show me a verse that proves that forsaking sin is not a mandate for salvation.

Okay. Take a look at 1 Peter 3:21.

The like figure whereunto even baptism doth also now save us (<u>not the putting away of the filth of the flesh,</u> but the answer of a good conscience toward God,) by the resurrection of Jesus Christ.

"Not putting away the filth of the flesh" is synonymous to "not forsaking sin" because without Christ, nothing can save you. Anyone who says that you have to forsake sin in order to be saved is expecting from you moral perfection. That's impossible and it furthermore contradicts this verse.

Romans 3:23.

For all have sinned, and come short of the glory of God.

Some use this verse to say, all <u>have</u> sinned, meaning past-tense sins.

But look at it again.

For all have sinned (past-tense), and come short (present-active tense) of the glory of God.

Nobody is sinfree!

And verse 24 should give us much consolation!

Being justified freely by his grace through the redemption that is in Christ Jesus.

So if you are a believer who is <u>struggling</u> with sin, you're definitely saved. The struggle confirms this.

Non-Christians don't struggle with sin; they just sin and won't even admit to having a sin problem in a non-facetious manner.

God bless.

23.No Condemnation.

(Textual Criticism.)

Romans 8:1.

Romans 8:1.
There is therefore now <u>no condemnation </u>to them which are in Christ Jesus, who walk not after the flesh, but after the Spirit.

Some of the OSFs will use this verse to subvert Sola Fide because they add an eisegetical qualifier. And the qualifier is this. There is no condemnation unto those who not only believe in Christ as Lord and Savior, but also to those who walk not after the flesh but after the spirit.

They can, in so doing, condemn anyone who purportedly doesn't walk after the spirit or those who walk after the flesh more than the spirit.

First of all, the latter phrase does not appear in some Greek manuscripts.

It does appear in the KJV, Geneva and other such derivative cognates like the NKJV or the 21CKJV, but some speculate that this was an erroneous typist error that was tautologically miscopied from 8 verse: 4.

In order that the righteous requirements of the law

might be fully met in us, who do not live according to the sinful nature but according to the Spirit.

Here is a list of some of the Bibles that have omitted the last ten words.

NIV.

NASB.

NLT.

ESV.

CEV.

NCV.

ASV.

TNIV.

I don't (at the time I originally wrote this manuscript) fanatically hold to the doctrine of KJV-onlyism. But I do prefer the anglicized King James 1611 as my favorite or choice version—especially when studying the Bible. I support "plenary verbal inspiration," a.k.a. majority text as opposed to minority texts. Too many good verses are omitted from the minority text Bibles. One pivotal one is…

Matthew 18:11.

For the Son of man is come to save that which was lost.

Why would anyone want to omit this verse from the Bible regardless of whether or not it was inferred to not have been in the original Greek manuscript? The inspired word of God is the inspired word of God. When I say "praise the Lord," "halleluiah" or "God is good," God inspired me to say it.

Romans 8:26.
Likewise the Spirit also helpeth our infirmities: for we know not what we should pray for as we ought: but the Spirit itself maketh intercession for us with groanings which cannot be uttered.

In other words, I wouldn't be able to produce anything <u>good</u>, whether it is rhetoric, prayer or just inner thoughts about God, without the assistance of the Holy Spirit. So, the inspired word of God is just that.

Another fraction of a verse that is omitted from minority text Bibles is the tail end of:

1 John 5:13.
These things have I written unto you that believe on the name of the Son of God; that ye may know that ye have eternal life, <u>and that ye may believe on the name of the Son of God.</u>

What this verse affirms in congruency with its preceding verses is that one may know that they have eternal life based on what is written.

According to minority text Bibles it stops there. (NIV, NLT). But if read from a majority text

Bible (KJV, ASV) one may know that they are saved and then with such unshakable knowledge — continue to believe. This reveals that we have eternal security and then encourages us to continue in our belief because of such a wonderful security.

I find that without eternal security it is hard to believe in God's infinite goodness and love, which then in turn inevitably causes man to put more confidence in his own works and volition — which is the epitome of pride!

Romans 8:1 says:

There is therefore now no condemnation to them which are in Christ Jesus. (Minority text).

Romans 8:1.
There is therefore now no condemnation to them which are in Christ Jesus, who walk not after the flesh, but after the Spirit. (Majority Text)

The omitted part can do two things. It can prove that a person is not saved if one doesn't walk after the spirit or it can prove that a person is saved if they do walk after the spirit.

This is a balance between pessimism and optimism, honesty and mendacity, works versus grace. And either stance is indeterminate. One would have to establish how much walking in the spirit would be enough to qualify his as being without condemnation and then conversely, how much walking after the flesh would qualify him for condemnation. We can't do this without being mistakenly subjective and guestimative.

One would even have to ask himself at all times if he or she is walking in the spirit or not—and honestly how would they even know?

Jeremiah 17:9.
The heart is deceitful above all things, and desperately wicked: who can <u>know</u> it?

My suggestion is to not question this as an absolute. I know that I am currently walking in the spirit because I can intuitively sense when the spirit is working in me. I also know when I am walking after the flesh. But neither recognition is completely black and white and in both polar cases there is much grayness. The bottom line is that if you are in Christ Jesus, there is therefore <u>now no condemnation</u>.

If you adhere to majority texts only, it is up to you whether you want to read something into the latter part of this verse. I'm not saying that in order to have eternal security we must relegate all our King James Bibles into desuetude and only read the minority text Bibles so that we can know we are saved whether we walk after the spirit or not.

I'm just suggesting that we don't read something into the text based on bias, prejudice or to a doctrinal inclination that may pervert the true message of the gospel, which is faith alone in Christ alone.

Let's take another look at both versions of Romans 8:1.

NIV.

Therefore, there is now no condemnation for those who are in Christ Jesus.

This says that if I am in Christ, there is no condemnation. Period.

KJV.

There is therefore now no condemnation to them which are in Christ Jesus, who walk not after the flesh, but after the Spirit.

This tells me that if I am in Christ there is now (at this very moment and forevermore) no condemnation. It also tells me that I should live after the spirit and not the flesh. It doesn't eternally condemn me if I do live after the flesh from time to time otherwise personal guilt, the need for confession, chastisement and the loss of eternal rewards would have no place or purpose.

Living after the flesh is just inevitable.

For my same Bible says that I can and will.

Matthew 26:41.
Watch and pray, that ye enter not into temptation: the spirit indeed is willing, but the flesh is weak.

John 3:6.

That which is born of the flesh is flesh; and that which is born of the Spirit is spirit.

Romans 7:18.

For I know that in me (that is, in my flesh,) dwelleth no good thing: for to will is present with me; but how to perform that which is good I find not.

1 Peter 2:11.

Dearly beloved, I beseech you as strangers and pilgrims, abstain from fleshly lusts, which war against the soul.

1 John 1:8.

If we say that we have no sin, we deceive ourselves, and the truth is not in us.

God bless.

24.Parable Of The Rich Young Ruler.

(Mark 10:17-22.)

Trying to save yourself by obeying the law just doesn't work. So many people think that they will get to heaven by being good. This is a lie from Satan. Nobody does good in God's eye without the Holy Spirit.

Romans 3:12.

They are all gone out of the way, they are together become unprofitable; there is none that doeth good, no, not one.

The idea that man is inherently good is a lie from Satan. It is the very reason people won't be saved. Because they can't see a need for a savior. Why throw somebody a lifejacket if they don't realize they are drowning? In such a case, they would be reluctant to receive it. For they would see no need for it.

Take a look at the parable of the rich young ruler.

Mark 10:17-22.

And when he was gone forth into the way, there came one running, and kneeled to him, and asked him, Good Master, what shall I do that I may inherit eternal life? And

Jesus said unto him, Why callest thou me good? there is none good but one, that is, God. Thou knowest the commandments, Do not commit adultery, Do not kill, Do not steal, Do not bear false witness, Defraud not, Honour thy father and mother. And he answered and said unto him, Master, all these have I observed from my youth. Then Jesus beholding him loved him, and said unto him, One thing thou lackest: go thy way, sell whatsoever thou hast, and give to the poor, and thou shalt have treasure in heaven: and come, take up the cross, and follow me. And he was sad at that saying, and went away grieved: for he had great possessions.

It sounds like Jesus is making salvation so bounden and contingent upon works that no one has a chance to avail himself or herself to it. Some might even surmise that this verse is a call to discipleship. But the point of this parable is to reveal to the rich young ruler what was not saving him.

Back up to verse 19.

Thou knowest the commandments, Do not commit adultery, Do not kill, Do not steal, Do not bear false witness, Defraud not, Honour thy father and mother.

Neither obeying the commandments nor observing them can save anyone. The rich young ruler mistakenly thought that he was "salvation material" because he observed the commandments.

And he answered and said unto him, Master, all these have I observed from my youth.

But Jesus was trying to let him know that that

wasn't good enough.

Good enough for what?

To be saved.

No.

To reign with Him in heaven.

The rich young ruler wasn't aware that he was a sinner and needed to come to Christ in faith to be saved. So Jesus went on to reveal that even though you observe the laws, you still have a wicked heart.

One thing thou lackest: go thy way, sell whatsoever thou hast, and give to the poor, and thou shalt have treasure in heaven: and come, take up the cross, and follow me. And he was sad at that saying, and went away grieved: for he had great possessions.

Jesus was making it crystal clear that this man was still wicked at heart and the proof was that he wasn't willing to give up his possessions, he wasn't willing to give to the poor, etc, etc. If the rich young ruler would have realized that he was wicked based on Jesus' latter words, he could have come to Him by simple faith and been saved.

Jesus wasn't raising the bar by telling him to divest himself and take up his cross. He was showing man's depravity and thus the only way to be saved. Know you're a sinner and believe on Jesus Christ for salvation!

This parable gets confused in so many ways to suggest that man must give up everything in order to be saved. How absurd. The point of this parabolic language was to reveal the rich young ruler's motive. In his own understanding, he wasn't that bad of a person. Christ's hyperbolic words were simply to show the condition of his heart. But to suggest that this parable gives us guidelines as to how we are supposed to live in order to be saved is not true.

I don't personally know of any Christians that have given up their house, car, job, money and luxuries in order to be saved. Such promoters of this breed of Lordship Salvation have made themselves into out-and-out hypocrites.

Saint Francis of Assisi was the exception not the rule.

God bless.

25.Not Of Works.

The rumors that are prevalently circulating around the world that salvation is by works are vast.

All secular religions are about works.

Karma, nirvana, pilgrimages to Mecca, offering oblations to idols, being ideally reincarnated, purgatory, keeping the law.

But the problem is that even modern day Christianity is fraught with this poison.

Catholics, Protestants, evangelicals. And even the cultist denominations. Mormons, Jehovah's Witnesses, Seven day Adventists, United Pentecostals, Church of Christ.

The message is not always overt.

Sometimes it's implicit.

I hear the message in twofold.

When I speak of works I'm also including sinlessness. That is a work in and of itself.

Think about it. If man could be justified by not sinning, but claim that they are not justified by works, how is not sinning any different when it takes work to refrain from sin?

Like installing a content-barrier on your computer to keep yourself from viewing pornography. Forcing yourself against your appetite to not eat any more potato chips by slapping your hand in self-admonition. That's work!

The message is either if you're not "doing such and such," then you haven't yet been saved.

Or...

If you are not "doing such and such" then you are proving that you aren't truly saved.

Both messages implicitly are exactly the same.

They both involve and require works.

In one case you are working to get saved or stay saved, in the other you are working to establish proof for salvation. In both cases, works are necessary.

You'll hear people say that good works just prove that you're saved.

So, are Muslims proving that they are saved by their works?

Works don't prove anything!

How about the atheists that donate to charities?

Bearing spiritual fruit however is a different story.

Galatians 5:22-23.

But the fruit of the Spirit is love, joy, peace,

longsuffering, gentleness, goodness, faith, Meekness, temperance: against such there is no law.

Love.

Joy.

Peace.

Longsuffering.

Gentleness.

Goodness.

Faith.

Meekness.

Temperance.

None of these fruit of the Spirit have any inherent work in them. They may motivate us to work or help us through our work, they may even keep us from sinning, but they do not attribute work to salvation.

You can be joyful without working and you can be full of peace and be a couch potato. You can bear all nine fruit paralyzed on your deathbed. I asked a Catholic if he believed in postmortem evangelism, thus explaining what I meant.

"Can a person be saved after they physically die?"

His response was profound, but nevertheless

contradicted by his qualification for salvation. He said that God is merciful and forgiving enough to save someone even after they physically die. But then he said that a person who claims to be saved but doesn't live for God is not saved. How can a person attain salvation after death and then be expected to live a certain way when he is dead? It is no different than the thief on the cross who was saved simply by faith, namely: asking to be remembered.

Works are excluded because Christ did all the work.

Romans 5:19.
For as by one man's disobedience many were made sinners, so by the obedience of one (Christ) shall many be made righteous (saved).

It is Christ's obedience that makes us righteous, even when we are filthy sinners, otherwise it would require our obedience.

I know workaholics that aren't even saved. Anyone trying to save themselves by their good works is just as lost as the God-rejecters. Because until you turn to Christ in simple faith, you have rejected Him.

Here's what scripture says about works.

Works would inevitably lead to boasting.

Romans 3:27.
Where is boasting then? It is excluded. By what law? of works? Nay: but by the law of faith.

It is excluded by faith.

What does boasting accomplish? Nothing, for it is an act of pride.

Obadiah 1:4.
Though thou exalt thyself as the eagle, and though thou set thy nest among the stars, thence will I bring thee down, saith the LORD.

But what about those that try to work for salvation without boasting or exalting themselves?

You can't. Somebody has to get the glory. It's either God or man.

1 Corinthians 1:31.

That, according as it is written, He that glorieth, let him glory in the Lord.

Works for salvation is man glorying in man!

Next time someone tries to take credit in their salvation, ask them to show you the nail holes and the laceration marks — or the piercing in their side. The reason so many well-intended people, even true Christians put an emphasis on works is because they like doing things for God and don't like the idea of our works being worthless. Our works aren't worthless if we are doing them for the right reason — for instance to earn eternal rewards.

But when we try to save ourselves by works, we make a travesty of Christ's finished work on the cross.

Salvation is not what man does, but by what Christ did. It's not by what man is doing, but by Christ's death at Calvary!

If you have come to Christ by faith alone and then through God's grace do good deeds, then your efforts are commendable and shall earn rewards in heaven! If works come from any other motive, like earning salvation, they are decidedly a disgrace.

Think about it.

God gives us grace.

We refuse the grace by trying to earn salvation.

We haven't accepted grace.

It becomes dis-grace!

****

Let me analogize.

You're getting ready to lose your house; it is shabby, unstable and uninhabitable. Not only is it impending to be foreclosed but also taken by ruination. I'm a master fixer-upper. I toil vigorously to fix it. I build an understructure, seal leaks, refenestrate, scrub walls and floors, detoxify, revamp the exterior, and reinstall the electricity, water and AC. I purge the house from all pestilence. Repaint it, add fixtures, and remove obstacles. I fix the plumbing system, reinsulate, and implement two roach-bombs. In the process, I get myriad splinters, cuts, scrapes, bruises, contusions, pockmarks, lacerations, internal bleeding, exhaustion, nausea, fatigue, major headaches and vertigo.

You come back and enjoy a repristinated house that is now perfectly immaculate. Would you have the temerity to say that you did some of the work? First of all, it would be a boldfaced lie. Second, it would rob me of the credit and third, it cheapens what has been done.

It would be as silly to say that while Mr. Fixer-upper was sacrificing blood, sweat and tears in laboring to fix my house, I was somehow contributing by covering my mouth when I coughed at the beach.

This is how insulting it is to think that we have anything to do with our salvation. I can imagine standing before Mr. Fixer-upper and him asking me why I should enjoy the house he just refurbished.

A humble, honest response would be: "Because, you fixed it up for me. Because you did all the work! You secured it, detoxified it and made it wonderfully livable!"

That would be the response of the honest Christian who understands grace.

The workists on the other hand will have to reply with:

"Uh, … you did do some of the work, but I covered my mouth while I coughed at the beach."

First of all, covering your mouth when you cough has nothing to do with living in the house and enjoying it.

Imagine standing before God on Judgment Day and God asks you why you should enter heaven. My response is going to have to be: Jesus Christ!

The workists may say because I swept my floor and did the dishes.

God will have to say. "Okay, but how does that have anything to do with the Kingdom of Heaven? You can't bring those dirty dishes into heaven.

The workist may reply with well I was good and gave up this sin and that.

God will reply: "Yeah but while you gave up this sin and that, Christ gave up His life to remove that sin from you forensically."

If your reply is not Jesus and Jesus alone, you still don't get it.

Romans 4:4.
Now to him that worketh is the reward not reckoned of grace, but of debt.

Working for salvation is implying that you owe God something for His precious gift that can only be received by grace alone through faith alone in

Christ alone! It also implies that God owes you! What a terrible position to be in!

God bless.

26.10 Things Happen When Christians Sin.

The Good News of the Bible is that we are saved by faith alone in Christ alone. That's the theme of this book. But so many Works Salvationists will label my theology "cheap grace" or "antinomianism" or "Licence-to-sinism," or whatever. I don't support such childish misnomers. This subset will assure you that as a Christian you cannot sin with impunity or without punitive consequences. Here are 10 things that happen to a Christian when he or she sins. In no respective order.

1. We temporarily break fellowship with God.

Psalm 51:12.
Restore unto me the joy of thy salvation; and uphold me with thy free spirit.

David had committed fornication with Bathsheba and conspired to have Uriah killed. He knew he was still saved and simply desired the joy of his salvation back.

2. We become ashamed.

Genesis 3:10.
And he said, I heard thy voice in the garden, and I was afraid, because I was naked; and I hid myself.

When Adam sinned in eating the forbidden fruit, he became ashamed. So ashamed that he hid himself and feared God.

3. We get chastised.

Hebrews 12:8.
But if ye be without chastisement, whereof all are partakers, then are ye bastards, and not sons.

When we sin, God chastises us. Plain and simple. This is how he brings us back into fellowship with Him.

4. We lose rewards in heaven.

1 Corinthians 3:15.
If any man's work shall be burned, he shall suffer loss: but he himself shall be saved; yet so as by fire.

We will lose rewards in heaven if we sin. Not salvation. Just rewards. Otherwise there would be no way to measure how rewards will be meted out.

5. We grieve the Holy Spirit.
Ephesians 4:30.
And grieve not the holy Spirit of God, whereby ye are sealed unto the day of redemption.

When we sin, we grieve or frustrate the Holy Spirit.

6. We become grieved.

Hebrews 12:11.
Now no chastening for the present seemeth to be

joyous, but grievous: nevertheless afterward it yieldeth the peaceable fruit of righteousness unto them which are exercised thereby.

When we sin we become grieved. Chastisement is not joyous, but always grievous as scripture affirms. In my not-so humble opinion there is no such thing as a practicing sinful Christian who is constantly, immutably happy. That is a contradiction of terms. And furthermore there is no such thing as a Christian that doesn't sin, otherwise who is being chastened in this verse?

7. We expedite physical death.

1 Corinthians 5:5.
To deliver such an one unto Satan for the destruction of the flesh, that the spirit may be saved in the day of the Lord Jesus.

When we persist in unrepentant sin, we draw ourselves closer to physical death. Romans 6:23. Romans 8:13. If we are lost, sin will draw us closer to spiritual, eternal death!

8. We ruin our witness.

1 John 3:8.
He that committeth sin is of the devil; for the devil sinneth from the beginning. For this purpose the Son of God was manifested, that he might destroy the works of the devil.

When we sin we identify ourselves with the devil. This is not a verse that describes which side we are on. God's or Satan's. This is referring to what we are identifying ourselves as. God's child or somebody who is acting like the devil's child. Jesus called Peter: Satan. (Matthew 16:23.) Yet Peter was still a saved disciple.

9. We lose subjective assurance of salvation.

2 Peter 1:10.
Wherefore the rather, brethren, give diligence to make your calling and election sure: for if ye do these things, ye shall never fall.

We can't lose salvation and we can't negate eternal security no matter how much we sin. (Hebrews 7:25, 1 John 2:1. Romans 5:20.) Eternal security is objective. Assurance of salvation is subjective. We can in our own mind's eye lose this assurance. However the reality and effectiveness of our eternal security can never be lost. Romans 8:38-39. John 6:37. Hebrews 9:12.

10. We necessitate confession.
Numbers 5:7
Then they shall confess their sin which they have done: and he shall recompense his trespass with the principal thereof, and add unto it the fifth part thereof, and give it unto him against whom he hath trespassed.

When we sin we shame ourselves to the point where we will not feel worthy even to pray. A confession is necessary in order to restore fellowship with God.

Notice that I did not include the eleventh

mythical: loss of salvation. Because that can never happen. If one could lose salvation because of sinning, the above ten consequences would cease to exist. Nor would they be necessary.

There would be no need for chastisement. No need for confession. No need to feel shameful. No need to lose rewards — if salvation could be lost.

Scripture confirms that when we are saved we are a child of God! A child of God cannot be unborn!

Galatians 3:26.
For ye are all the children of God by faith in Christ Jesus

God bless.

27.Who are the pretenders?

Lots of people would say that those who have unrepentant sin in their life or those who "play Christian," yet live a hypocritical life elsewhere are the pretenders. But we must be remindful that everyone puts on a façade from the moment they enter the church till the moment they are back into the private confines of their own abode. The question is how much of the façade flakes off during this transition?

Hopefully, it doesn't go from prim and proper to rude and crude. For me, it just goes from pretending not to covet to actually coveting.

But who are the pretenders?

The pretenders are those who are trusting in their own goodness or good works to save them. You will easily be able to spot them based on their skewed idea of salvation. They will add to the free grace message the Bible clearly proclaims.

Romans 5:18.
Therefore as by the offence of one judgment came upon all men to condemnation; even so by the righteousness of one the free gift came upon all men unto justification of life.

The only ways to not be saved are to just say no to this free gift or to try to earn it yourself. The latter is oxymoronic. You can't earn a gift! We need to listen for such statements:

1. It can't be that easy.

2. There must be more to it.

3. You gotta add repentance.

4. You have to compare scripture to scripture.

5. You gotta really believe.

6. That's just cheap grace or easy-Believism.

7. Salvation is a genuine transformation.)

All such rhetoric is simply a byproduct of unbelief!

As a saved, believer I can honestly say to the following statements about salvation.

1. It is that easy!

2. There's nothing more to it.

3. No repentance is necessary.

4. No scriptural comparison is necessary.

5. Believing is really believing. Or what does it mean to really believe?

6. It's free grace and I don't have a problem with easy-Believism.

7. Salvation is by grace through faith in Christ.

A person can think that they are not saved until blue in the face. They may be basing such ill thoughts on their sins or their wicked imagination or because their good deeds seem to underweigh their bad deeds. But this has nothing to do with whether or not they have accepted the free gift.

Such negative thoughts can either block you from receiving the free gift of salvation or they can cause you to forget that you have received it thus stifling your joy. So, does a pattern of sinfulness qualify someone as a pretender? As surprising as this may seem, the so-called sinful hypocrite is probably more justified than the prideful people in our churches that act as if they don't sin. Sadly, those are who I suspect to be the pretenders.

There's hope for the habitual sinner, and that hope is spiritual growth. But there is no hope for the man that can look in the mirror and see virtual sinlessness. He's looking in the wrong mirror!

The Bible says to grow in grace. (2 Peter 3:18.)

Grace is the remedy for sin.

If we don't see our sins, we can't activate the remedy.

A pretender is simply someone who hasn't accepted grace as a free gift. Such a person knows nothing of grace. I've heard Christians basically imply that a Christian had to live a certain way and they raised the bar so high that nobody living in sinful reality could attain it. This is an entire removal of grace. They may act as if they've given another definition to grace, which is specious. But to give grace any other meaning is simply to abolish it.

Anyone who prides himself in his own performance even if he claims that God demands it is grossly deceived. If God demanded holiness from us, he would have erred in making grace free. God simply wants to see his grace procured and then glow from His children naturally.

Demanded holiness knows nothing of grace. Grace doesn't demand holiness. Holiness should just automatically emanate from grace without a demand. I can see holiness rearing to show itself in the life of a Christian but then halting at a regulatory sign posted with the following words: "I demand holiness!" The holiness wants to shine forth freely, but because of such harsh enforcement, it no longer can. I could imagine such a stream of holiness doing a U-turn at this legalistic demand and then falling into a recession of stagnancy.

Analogically speaking, imagine the love of my life running to me with ardor and a huge nonpareil smile, her arms spread-eagle. She's impending to give me the biggest and most epical hug in the world. Freely, openly, unforced, willingly, lovingly, expressly. I open my arms and freely embrace her! The hug enlocks! This is the perfect picture!

Now let me paint this scenario again with the

idea of demanded holiness. Imagine the love of my life running to me with ardor and a huge nonpareil smile—her arms spread-eagle. She's impending to give me the biggest and most epical hug in the world. Freely, openly, unforced, willingly, lovingly, expressly. Right before she embraces me, I drop my arms, capsize my smile into an evil, clownish smirk, whip a gun out of my pocket and, like a rapist, demand a hug! This epitomizes absurdity for she was willing to hug me without a coercive threat! This is a facsimile of saying that God demands holiness.

Some say it and actually believe that they are honoring God by such a statement, but the truth of the matter is that they are simply lauding themselves from a standpoint that is deeply mired in pride and self-righteousness!

What about this verse?

Now by this we know that we know Him, if we keep His commandments. (1 John 2:3.)

Bob Wilkin expounds:

Imagine hearing this statement about a man who had just divorced his wife of many years, "They were married for thirty years and yet he never knew her." He certainly knew his wife in one sense. She had been his wife for thirty years. However, he did not know her in the sense of *intimate fellowship knowledge.* So it is with carnal Christians and their knowledge of God.

This is simply a verse that describes being in fellowship with God. That requires obedience, but still such obedience is not demanded, it is optional. The Bible is full of examples of Christians that fell out of fellowship with God. Discipleship and salvation are two totally different things.

Hebrews 12:14.
Follow peace with all men, and holiness, without which no man shall see the Lord.

Following holiness, which is Christ, is a far cry difference from being holy with our own efforts. This scripture is simply exhorting us to keep following Christ—He is our only hope and our holiness.

God bless.

28.Pride. A Subtle Deception.

There's a subtle deception out there that at first seems admirable. But after much prayerful deliberation, I've finally caught on. Usually when someone hears something, a word for instance, they don't catch on to its' subtext right away. When the word is repeated twice, they may catch on, but consequently they may not. But after hearing it thrice, they should thereof have a full grasp of what is *really* being stated. Let me explain this subtle deception.

Whether before salvation or after matters not…

Listen to the following statements…

"We need to commit ourselves to Christ."

"We need to make Christ our Lord and Savior."

"We need to obey God."

What was the recurring word?

"We."

We … we … we.

I hope that you can see where the focal point is.

It is on man. It's all about what man does. Commit himself, make Christ his Lord and Savior, obey God, etc!

Such commands are awash in self-centered pride.

First of all, man doesn't make Christ Lord. Christ is Lord upon faith.

Man doesn't make Christ the Savior. Christ is the Savior and He makes man saved!

Man doesn't make Christ anything! We are His creation. He is not ours. Christ is independently Lord and Savior and He doesn't need man's permission or his validation. All man can do is accept Christ on His terms.

This deception at first seems harmless enough. People that are adding anything to salvation by faith think that they are doing it out of humility. Nothing could be further from the truth. When man self-imposes obedience and then chides the disobedient, he is driven by pride. Such humility is shrouded by pride. A demand for obedience sounds sincere at first, but such a demand is steeped in self-righteousness and pride because man's motive for obedience is centered by man's inclination to obey God.

When I hear someone say that if they don't straighten up their act then they deserve to go to hell, I'm at first inclined to think that they are sincerely humble in making such a statement, but the more I think about it, the more I realize that this person is simply stressing a high emphasis on his own good works and obedience. With that being so, his so-called humility is exposed as being nothing more than sinful pride! Nothing less! Nothing more!

Man deserves to go to hell the way it is! Not because he won't, can't or refuses to straighten up his act. Such a prideful attempt to improve himself just makes him more deserving of hell.

If man doesn't let grace be grace, he will always be categorized this way. Instead of man demanding himself and others to obey God, man is humbler in just admitting that he doesn't obey God to best of his ability and needs to try harder.

Christ is the Savior.

Man is the sinner.

Pride oftentimes forgets this.

We should obey God, but we need to remember that such obedience is simply out of appreciation for grace.

The problem is not the intention behind such statements like: "obey God." The problem is the statement itself.

We need to tell people <u>how</u> to obey God. Not just to obey God. If I told a newbie Christian to obey God and left it at that, he would be confused and in wonderment as to how someone does this. I should give him ways or examples of obeying God. Like…

Read your Bible.

Attend church.

Memorize scripture.

Pray.

Fellowship in love with other Christians.

Evangelism.

Etc. etc.

God bless.

29. The Sin Delusion!

1 John 1:9.

If we confess our sins, He is faithful and just to forgive us our sins and to cleanse us from all unrighteousness.

Scripture doesn't say.

If we pretend to not sin that much, He is faithful and just to forgive us our sins and to cleanse us from all unrighteousness.

I've had my fill of this whole self-righteous, *I've-got-sin-under-control* garbage! It misses the point of salvation, grace, humility and confession. I don't have sin under control and neither do you! This mentality reveals that a person isn't as spiritually mature as they think they are. It also bears a false witness to others in terms of spiritual expectancy.

When one errs on thinking that they don't sin (that much) it causes many problems for those who do still struggle with sin. It makes them think that they must reach an equivalent level of righteousness in order to be saved or worthy of the title: Christian. This is a demonic ploy that Satan uses to dissuade newbie Christians from any form of Christocentric growth.

The victims feel that the bar has been set too high and that it is thereby impossible to live up to it. This needs to be extinguished from Christendom altogether. It is a sign of spiritual stagnancy, not growth! As we grow in Christ, we discover more and more just how sinful we are. (Romans 7:8.)

I've heard people say that they can go an entire day without sinning. If they were really growing spiritually, they'd know otherwise. And how can one make such a statement without puffing up with selfish pride?

As you read your Bible, pray and get divine revelation from God, you will discover that Christ shows you what it is that you are to be doing.

James 4:15. (NKJV.)

Instead you ought to say, "If the Lord wills, we shall live and do this or that.

This verse tells us that the Lord reveals His will to us and encourages us to obey Him.

How can we say that we don't sin daily? To not sin daily is to say "yes" to everything God tells you to do.

Knock on your neighbor's door and offer to buy him lunch. Pray for six straight hours, abstain from eating sweets; spend two hours each night in the Bible. Quit your job, do some pro bono work and just trust that God will monetarily take care of you. If you fail to do any of these things, you've sinned.

James 4:17.

Therefore to him that knoweth to do good, and doeth it not, to him it is <u>sin</u>.

That means that if I know I should add a few scriptures to this thesis and don't do it, I have deliberately sinned whilst writing this.

Take a look at:

Romans 6:12.
Let not sin therefore reign in your mortal body, that ye should obey it in the lusts thereof.

I heard someone assert that—as Christians—sin may dwell in us but it doesn't reign in us. This is a moot point in which later he contradicted by saying that it <u>shouldn't</u> reign in us. This scripture is an exhortation not to let sin reign in your mortal body. It isn't proclaiming that it won't.

Now, here's the hair-splitter.

First of all, no one can determine the difference between, "dwelling" and "reigning" for they are subjective dubbings for quantifying sin. What constitutes *sin dwelling in you* versus sin *reigning in you*? Nobody knows. Because for everyone it is something different. Hypothetically speaking, I look at porn twice a day, but that just proves that sin *dwells* in me. If I viewed it seven times a day that would constitute sin *reigning* in me. Now, for my neighbor, he only looks at porn once a week and he considers that to be sin *reigning in him*. See, such subjectivity makes differentiating the two sin nuances an impossibility.

Some may say that sin doesn't reign in them it just maximally dwells in them or that sin doesn't dwell in them it just minimally reigns in me! This is an issue that leads to much indetermination and inconclusive hair-splitting.

Forsaking sins is not the gospel nor is it part of the gospel.

You didn't do anything to save yourselves and you don't do anything to keep yourselves saved.

Sin dwelling and sin reigning are no different and neither is excusable.

Sin reigning ... I had to do it!

Sin dwelling ... I didn't have to do it but I did it anyway!

Bottom-line is that YOU DID IT!

I don't see much of a difference.

God bless.

30. Turn From Sin.

W.I.S.C.

When I read gospel tracts that say, "turn from sin," what I envisage is the reader laughing to himself, wadding the tract up and then TURNING FROM GOD! That's all this crazy heresy does. If I had to turn from sin in order to be saved, as a lost heathen, I would have done the same thing. Even now, as a regenerate, Holy Spirit-filled Christian, I would probably at least frown upon the tract with a sense of hopelessness and confusion.

The only person, who would read a Chick Tract, smile and then say the sinner's prayer with the notion that he in fact did turn from his sins, is a deceived, self-righteous person that perhaps doesn't even realize what his sins are. Even our good deeds are sinful according to scripture.

Psalm 39:5.

Behold, thou hast made my days as an handbreadth; and mine age is as nothing before thee: verily every man at his best state is altogether vanity. Selah.

This "turn from sins" message is probably the subtlest of all deceptions. The gospel seems clear when faith alone in Christ alone is proclaimed, but when the "turn from sin" part comes up the clarity and simplicity of the gospel is morbidly vitiated.

Someone will or should ask how turning from

sins is even possible. This is misleading. Those who shout, "turn from sins" are wolves in sheep's clothing or otherwise just ignorant of the gospel, which makes them a self-unaware W.I.S.C.

First of all, this false message makes the gospel seem serial. The reader of such a tract might feel as if he needs to trust in Christ for salvation as step one, then he must give up his bad habits (sins) as step two, … three … and four.

For instance.

Step one: faith in Christ.

Step two: give up smoking.

Step three: give up drinking.

Step four: give up cheating on taxes.

After he realizes that he can't give them up, he feels that salvation is an impossible waste of time — at least for him. And then he angrily rebels against God even more vehemently. I know people who think being a Christian means not sinning at all. And they have vocally expressed that it was impossible to be a Christian. And they have such deceptive "turn from sin" tracts and teachings to thank for this false notion.

Street preachers with the "turn from sin" message are not delivering the message of salvation, but are bringing the message of damnation. The free grace message is both. It is that salvation is free for anyone who wants it. (Revelation 21:6.) Those who reject it and keep on rejecting it until they die will be damned. But salvation was still nevertheless free. The "turn from sin" street preachers are giving no hope. They scream turn from your sin in order to be saved and the Bible emphatically speaks against this.

John 15:5.
I am the vine, ye are the branches: He that abideth in me, and I in him, the same bringeth forth much fruit: for <u>without me ye can do nothing</u>.

The street preachers are implying that those they witness to are lost, unregenerate, and without Christ. Scripture is clear that without Christ man can do nothing. Jesus, Himself even said that He could do nothing without the Father's help.

John 8:28.
Then said Jesus unto them, When ye have lifted up the Son of man, then shall ye know that I am he, and that I do nothing of myself; but as my Father hath taught me, I speak these things.

His disciples even recognized this.

John 9:33.
If this man were not of God, he could do nothing.

The Bible is clear that with God nothing is impossible.

Luke 1:37.
For with God nothing shall be impossible.

This means that without God nothing is POSSIBLE!

The "turn from sin" demand is a biblical impossibility for the unregenerate person. But then you have some real sly deceivers that will say this. Yes, it is impossible to turn from sins before you are saved but after you've received the Holy Spirit, you will have the power to overcome sin. And if you are still sinning you must not really have the Holy Spirit; hence you must not be saved at all.

This is bogus!

Scripture is clear that we do sin as Christians. When we do this; we quench the spirit.

1 Thessalonians 5:19.
Quench not the Spirit.

If having the indwelt Holy Spirit meant that we had the power to turn from sin and that—this turning from sin was a guarantee—why would scripture warn us not to quench the spirit? Furthermore why would the Bible give exhortations to live after the spirit if it were an automatic guarantee?

Galatians 5:16.
This I say then, Walk in the Spirit, and ye shall not fulfil the lust of the flesh.

The idea that true Christians will all turn from sin and walk in the spirit invariably after conversion is a manmade lie. Most Christians don't walk in the spirit the way they should. The Bible is full of exhortations to live a spiritual life. If the spiritual life after conversion were a preset guarantee, then why would the Bible give us instructions on how to live?

The scripture would have to read.

Galatians 5:16.
This I say then, you automatically Walk in the Spirit, and you do not fulfil the lust of the flesh.

Nowhere in scripture does it say that Christians automatically turn from sins and live by the aegis of the Holy Spirit. Those who say that you are not a real Christian unless you live in the Spirit and forsake your sins have changed the gospel message and frustrated grace. They are deceivers, liars and heretics. (Galatians 1:6-9, 2:21.)

You can't add any qualifications to the free grace gospel message because all qualifications are unquantifiable. Nobody knows how much spirituality it would take to prove that a person is saved after faith so no one can define this so-called "true faith." The Bible says that all you must have is the faith of a mustard seed — and not even that. Such a faith can move a mountain.

Well I haven't seen any mountains being deracinated and then hovering high in the sky ready to be dunked into the ocean. So, even mustard-seed-faith is not being expressed in order to be saved. I can only conclude that less-than-mustard-seed faith is enough to get saved.

The bottom line is that the Bible makes it clear. If a person wants to be saved, it's as easy as pie. Just believe in Jesus for the promise of eternal life. It is a damnable heresy to add anything to such a simple invitation. Telling people to turn from their sins in order to be saved is a lie from the pits of hell. Telling people that after they are saved they have to turn from sins in order to prove that they are saved is another lie from the pits of hell.

After a person is saved, God may or may not deliver His children from a particular sin. But this is the work of God, not man.

Philippians 2:13.
For it is God which worketh in you both to will and to do of his good pleasure.

The only thing man can do is to let God do the works in him. We do this by feeding ourselves spiritual food. We plant the seed — praying, Bible-reading, soul winning, listening to sermons — God produces the spiritual harvest. God bought us so that He could work in us. This scripture says that it is not only God who works in us but it is God who wills in us.

"Turn from sins," as a means of salvation is a Satanic lie from hell and must be repudiated!

The only way for us to do anything righteous is to be born again.

1 John 2:29.

If ye know that he is righteous, ye know that every one that doeth righteousness is <u>born of him.</u>

So the next time you hear someone demand that you must turn from your sins in order to be saved, ask him or her why they haven't turned from their own self-righteous, deceptive heresy.

God bless.

31.Power Of God.

One denominator in the anti-free grace movement is negativism.

Anyone that denies free grace and preaches against it is a heretic. Such denials may not be patent and some deny free grace in one field of thought but accept it in another. You will be able to detect a denier of free grace when they try to tell you what grace is. They may say that grace is the ability to obey God or grace is what enables you to stop sinning. Well these sound like good answers but they fall short as to what grace is in its entire essence.

True grace may enable you to obey God, but it is much more than just that. Those that have denied free grace and made grace seem like an obedience-enabler are trying to shove their works-theology down your throat. Rephrase them in excess and you will get this.

"Grace is the ability to obey God and if you aren't obeying God you don't have grace! You're not saved."

They have simply turned grace into works which Romans 11:6 forbids. Such people would be perfectly happy if the word "grace" was completely omitted from their Bible in every area of scripture. They would be utterly delighted not to see the word "grace" in their Bible at all. It would therefore lend more gravitas to their damnable works heresy.

But because grace is found in the Bible many times, they simply frown on it and have to change its definition insofar that it is no longer grace at all.

In fact, if you could fraudulently forge a new translation of the Bible that read, "You are saved by works, not grace…" I'm sure you could sell hundreds of copies to works-minded people that have in effect denied the power of God. Such people are quick to condemn sinners and hate free grace. Just like Satan.

Their whole mentality is deeply mired in negativism. A works Salvationist in my opinion is a spiritual crook or spiritual rapist. They are simply espousing salvific impossibility and a false reason to brag about their own good works. I have no respect for a works Salvationist because they are sick people who usually become sicker and sicker overtime.

I've heard one say that God will forgive you of small accidental sins but not if you make a practice of sin. A few weeks later he asserted that you have to literally be perfect or else you won't get to heaven. The verse he quoted refers to Christ's imputed perfection by faith alone, yet he was evoking the idea of human perfection. See how his theology has atrophied. It went from a teaspoon of grace that covered accidental sins to no-grace, which explained the only way to justify his definition of, "perfect."

He later went on condemning people to hell that had physical handicaps on the basis of the handicap. Months before that he was condemning infants and children to hell. He also claimed that nobody could know if they were the true elect. It's just one sick ideology after another.

Opponents of free grace are warped, not well intentioned with just differences of opinions, but warped! They twist and jockey scripture out of context to a morbid degree. This needs to be stopped and such people need to be avoided, prayed for and loved yes, but outright avoided!

Such people have denied the power of God.

1 Corinthians 1:18.

For the preaching of the cross is to them that perish foolishness; but unto us which are saved it is the power of God.

To a denier of free grace this scripture applies. If you deny free grace you are perishing because without grace you aren't saved. If you aren't saved you are perishing—hence the cross is foolish to you.

Romans 1:16.

For I am not ashamed of the gospel of Christ: for it is the power of God unto salvation to every one that believeth; to the Jew first, and also to the Greek.

The power of God. Salvation by free grace is only certain because it is God who saves and His power alone that saves us.

What have the deniers of free grace done?

They've denied the power of God.

2 Timothy 3:5.

Having a form of godliness, but denying the power thereof: from such turn away.

The verse before this, 4, is referring to traitors, heady and high-minded people, but I believe that it is also referring to anyone that denies the power of God. Scripture is clear that God saves us by His grace. So if we deny free grace as many do, then we deny our only means of salvation. We may even have the appearance of godliness. Trying to save yourself with your own works is simply accrediting your own works and unwittingly in lieu of God's power.

We are only saved and even strong in our walk because of God.

2 Samuel 22:33.
God is my strength and power: and he maketh my way perfect.

Deniers of free grace have valued their own power over God's. How do I know this? Simple. When they demand that we must do something to be saved apart from faith alone and then condemn one another for not doing it, they are implying that our deeds in our power are putting us in eternal peril. They can't say that God enables us to do good deeds because they would be condemning God's enabling power if such good deeds were lacking.

Psalm 62:11.
God hath spoken once; twice have I heard this; that power belongeth unto God.

Conclusion.

After much rumination about everything I know about God, myself, my sins, the Bible, my life, the lives of others and any other thing I can think of or talk about I've come to one universal and immutable conclusion. Every human being alive is absolutely doomed without Jesus Christ.

Everyone without exception.

Now, I'm not implying that such people as handicapped, children, infants and undomesticated people don't inherently have Jesus and are hopeless, but I am implying that all who consciously reject Christ are! But in keeping with free grace, those who reject free grace are in essence rejecting Christ at least in terms of salvific implementation.

Think about it, if Christ is our only hope, but you reject free grace then you are giving a false hope. If coming to Christ is not enough and every opponent of free grace must hold to this, then we are without hope.

I am, you are, everyone is!

No exceptions!

Denying free grace is essentially how a religious person stays lost! Anyone, who at one time did believe free grace theology but has now stopped, they have committed true apostasy and need to repent and return home.

32.Discipleship Versus Salvation.

Some people hold to a view that denies the fact that some Christians—saved by grace—are not disciples. They make salvation and discipleship one and the same. In other words, if you are not living spiritually, then you are not saved, according to their view. This denies the fact that there are carnal Christians at large. According to Paul's dealings with the church of Corinth there were. Some people have the audacity to suggest that these Christians weren't yet saved. But what does scripture clearly say.

1 Corinthians 3:1.
And I, brethren, could not speak unto you as unto spiritual, but as unto carnal, even as unto babes in Christ.

<u>In Christ.</u>

It appears that these Christians were carnal, unworthy of the title: disciple.

Is a lazy, carnal, adolescent saved if he has accepted salvation by faith alone in Christ alone? YES. But would you consider him a disciple? Not hardly. In scripture, disciples are always given a command. And although we still sin, disciples are called to a higher living.

Matthew 8:23.
And when he was entered into a ship, his disciples followed him.

This was literal in the Bible sense of time and is figurative for us as Christians today. How do we follow Jesus today, one may be wondering? Read our Bible, pray, attend church, evangelize, love one another. Being a slothful deadbeat is not synonymous to following Christ. To suggest or require all Christians to be disciples in order to be saved is a distortion of the gospel and unbiblical.

True, we all should follow Christ as disciples but not everyone does.

Matthew 25:26.
His lord answered and said unto him, Thou wicked and slothful servant, thou knewest that I reap where I sowed not, and gather where I have not strawed.

Also see: John 4:1.
To postulate that all Christians are disciples is to say that this servant in this parabolic context wasn't saved. That is not true because no lost person is considered a servant. The Old Testament is replete with the word "enemies" referring to the lost. Exodus 23:22.

Disciples are already saved.

John 8:31.
Then said Jesus to those Jews which <u>believed</u> on him, If ye continue in my word, then are ye my disciples indeed.

Notice the context. "Which believed on him." They were already believers before they were called to be disciples.

The message of salvation is John 3:16.

Discipleship is a matter of spiritual growth. Ignore those who fuse discipleship and salvation together.

The condition of salvation is believing in Jesus. A onetime act of faith alone in Christ alone. The condition of discipleship is *continuing in my word.*

God bless.

33.Fellowship With God.

What is it and how do we know if we are in it?

Fellowship with God is not salvation. Salvation is a free gift. (Romans 6:23.) Fellowship with God consists of walking in the spirit. How do we know if we are walking in the spirit? The Holy Spirit will dictate our actions. We will crave the word of God. (Matthew 4:4, 5:6.). We will pray. (Psalm 50:14, 1 Thessalonians 5:17.) We will crave church and delight in the love of God and others. (1 John 3:14.) Keep in mind, when I say church I am referring to a Bible-based church with sound, orthodox doctrine.

Is someone who doesn't pray, read his Bible, attend church or do other spiritual things in fellowship with God?

Resoundingly: NO!

1 John 1:6.

If we say that we have fellowship with him, and walk in darkness, we lie, and do not the truth.

This does not mean that we are not saved; it just means that we can't be in fellowship with God and live in sin at the same time. Let me illustrate. Imagine someone going to church and ardently praising God — at that time they are actively in fellowship with God. Yes. True fellowship.

However, they come home and immediately watch ungodly television for two hours or so. They have broken fellowship. They turn the TV off and read their Bible. Fellowship restored! Twenty-five minutes into Bible-reading they decide to look at Internet pornography. Fellowship broken! Such ebbs and flows are common for all Christians — so what do we do about it?

How do we maintain our fellowship?

Galatians 5:25.

If we live in the Spirit, let us also walk in the Spirit.

This just means doing spiritual things. I've listed the basics in the latter of this subset.

How do we restore our fellowship?

1 John 1:9.

If we confess our sins, he is faithful and just to forgive us our sins, and to cleanse us from all unrighteousness.

Confession is not how we maintain our fellowship; it is how we restore it. If confession was our maintenance then we would have to spend all our spiritual time confessing, the same sins over and over again.

Keep in mind that a Christian who is not in fellowship with God doesn't mean that he is lost or can lose his salvation. Salvation is free and cannot be lost, as I've emphasized heavily thus far. Fellowship is something we have to work on and this is simply done by the Holy Spirit.

Philippians 2:13.
For it is God which worketh in you both to will and to do of his good pleasure.

The spirit does the work in us but it is up to us not to grieve the spirit by neglecting spiritual things like: Bible reading, prayer, fasting, church, evangelism, memorizing scripture, etc, ... etc.

Fellowship with God is important for it is part of our spiritual growth. To neglect such a growth is putting us in peril for God chastens His children. Hebrews12:5-8.

God bless.

34.Sodom And Gomorrah.

Lordship Salvationists would condemn all the sodomites of Sodom and Gomorrah to hell, but were all the sodomites lost? Probably not. Some were saved like Lot. God was angry at Sodom and Gomorrah for they wouldn't relent in their sexual aberrations.

Genesis 18:20.

And the LORD said, Because the cry of Sodom and Gomorrah is great, and because their sin is very grievous.

Lordship Salvation has no grace and no forgiveness towards sinful sodomites. Prideful Christians would want all the homosexuals of this world to be lost and impending the damnation of hell. But does the Bible condemn all the sodomites in Sodom to hell?

Genesis 18:23.

And Abraham drew near, and said, Wilt thou also destroy the righteous with the wicked?

This verse says that some of the inhabitants of Sodom were righteous. But we must keep in mind that righteous in the Bible refers to the person's position, not experience.

Romans 10:10.

For with the heart man believeth unto righteousness;

and with the mouth confession is made unto salvation.

Righteousness is our positional standing when we are in Christ.

It is not referring to our conduct for we are all sinners. Some might say that the righteous weren't guilty of sodomy. Because righteousness was their positional standing one can only speculate as to whether there were true born-again sodomites in Sodom.

Take a look at the next verse.

Genesis 18:25.

That be far from thee to do after this manner, to slay the righteous with the wicked: and that the righteous should be as the wicked, that be far from thee: Shall not the Judge of all the earth do right?

This says that the righteous in their position were experientially behaving like the wicked sodomites. So, yes, some of the sodomites were saved.

Lot was a sodomite.

Genesis 19:33.

And they made their father drink wine that night: and the firstborn went in, and lay with her father; and he perceived not when she lay down, nor when she arose.

Some might say that Lot didn't have a choice; he was intoxicated against his will. Well hey. If that were the case, we could all just get drunk, lewd, debauched and vandalistic and then just blame it on the booze. Lot slept with his daughters, period. He even gave his daughters up to sodomites. (Genesis 19:8.) He was carnal! The Lordship Salvationists would condemn anyone who acted like Lot but the Bible calls Lot a just man.

2 Peter 2:6-8.

And turning the cities of Sodom and Gomorrah into ashes condemned them with an overthrow, making them an ensample unto those that after should live ungodly; And delivered just Lot, *vexed with the filthy conversation of the wicked. (For that righteous man dwelling among them, in seeing and hearing, vexed his righteous soul from day to day with their unlawful deeds.)*

On one side of the coin, Lot was an incestuous fornicator and on the other side of the coin, he was positionally righteous only because he was a believer in God.

Sodom and Gomorrah was a prophetic type of the rapture and the wrath upon the wicked during the tribulation.

Now don't get me wrong, I'm not condoning Sodomy or homosexuality, for both are heinous acts of sin against God. I'm simply avowing that our sinfulness has nothing to do with our position in Christ. Rehab was a harlot, Samson was a womanizer, David was a fornicator. All have sinned and come short of the glory of God.

Homosexuality is the causation of AIDS. Read on.

Romans 1:27.

And likewise also the men, leaving the natural use of the woman, burned in their lust one toward another; men with men working that which is unseemly, and receiving in themselves that recompense of their error which was meet.

Recompense of their error could mean a negative repercussion of sin in a manner that has nothing to do with disease, but it could very well mean venereal diseases like AIDS.

Sodomy is a horrible sin but grace does cover it.

God bless.

35.Salvation Is Allergic To Works.

So many people will say that if you add works to faith you don't have salvation. Now works without faith can't save you. We are saved by faith alone in Christ. To say that if you have placed genuine faith in Christ but then added works you aren't saved is erroneous for this mentality is just as austere as denying someone salvation without works. In other words, paradoxically, not adding works to salvation when man intrinsically has a propensity to do so in itself, is a work. It would be like me saying that you are saved by faith alone in Christ and if you have added to this Christ-aloneness you aren't really saved for the attempt to strive, maintain or sustain this aloneness without works has ironically became a work in disguise!

The best way to look at it is like this: you are saved by faith alone in Christ alone and when a person adds works to this they are sinning by selfishly and pridefully adding human effort to their salvation. This sin of "adding works" is covered by the Blood of Christ. Now, there are some people that have works and no faith, but to say that they don't have real faith unless they exclude works is simply miscategorizing a person's faith. One caveat: some who have added works are not saved at all and are still on their way to hell. Only God knows if a person has believed on Christ or not. The reason I'm adding this is because I know people that have believed in faith alone then latter down the years due to bad teaching changed their belief to faith plus perseverance or whatever.

The underlying issue is that we, as Christians, don't have personal faith detectors. So we can't know whether or not a person has real faith. It is not advisable to question whether a Mormon, Jehovah's Witness, Catholic, Protestant or even an evangelical has real faith in Christ based on anything they practice. Only God knows that; only He knows their heart.

The problem is not the church, assembly or denomination; the problem is pride. Every man has pride in him and that is why he adds works to his theology. It's not a Catholic problem or a Protestant problem. It's a pride problem. If you are saved by faith in Christ your pride-sin is covered. It is prideful to demand good works and it is likewise prideful to condemn those who have added works as though workfulness or worklessness were anymore taboo, one to the other.

Salvation is by faith in Christ without the works of the law. But man, because of his standing in grace, should want to do good works. When man gets confused as to whether he is working for salvation or from salvation, this sin of confusion is also forgiven. We must remember that what Christ did for us in order to pay the price for our sins is too great to be impeded by man's prideful confusion.

Most people add works to some degree!

So if those who have added works (out of ignorance) are on their way to hell, then God will be sending most people to hell. It's that simple. But how can I say that most people add works. Let me give you some paraphrased quotes.

If you don't endure to the end you aren't saved.

Catholic.

Faith and works are like two legs and without one you won't be able to stand up.

Protestant.

Faith will save you but it is only one ingredient in salvation. It's kind of like this, a plant needs water in order to live but it also needs sunlight, etc, etc.

Protestant.

Honestly, these statements have either blatantly or subtlety added works to salvation. Does this mean that a loving God would condemn his beloved children all because they got their semantics mixed up? No.

True, there are self-righteous people who don't love God and just want to condemn others to hell or give them no assurance of salvation out there that aren't saved and are children of the devil, which I fear, are on the broad path to hell, but not everyone who adds works to faith is in that camp. Some do it by accident; others do it to prompt spiritual growth. Some do it in order to substantiate their own assurance of salvation. And there are always those who just misunderstand the Bible. A person's heart needs to be examined in such a case.

Q: Why does man add works?

A: Pride.

It's hard for anyone to accept a gift freely without wanting to defray the giver. Someone comes up to you and hands you 100 dollars and the first thing you want to do is to give them something in return. If a Christian, Catholic or Protestant, has accepted the free gift of salvation and is doing good works out of appreciation—whether they've noted this appreciation in their doctrine or not—then they aren't doing a total harm in this confusion.

However if a person is just hell-bent on making sinners feel unsavable and themselves feel like sinless, sanctimonious perfectionists then they have a big problem and should be avoided like the plague.

Arminians say that if you don't do good works you will lose your salvation. Calvinists say that if you don't do good works, you just prove you never were saved. Both statements are implicitly saying the same thing. The goal is to practice free grace. Believe in free grace and ideological rid all works from your thinking.

I'm not saying that you shouldn't do good works; I'm saying that where the words: *salvation* and *justification* are, you MUST remove "works" from your vocabulary.

The statement below is even erroneous.

"Faith will naturally produce good works."

Faith is how you attained salvation and if salvation is not of works then why are you putting the word 'work' or 'works' in a sentence that has "faith" in it.

Galatians 2:16.

Knowing that a man is not justified by the works of the law, but by the faith of Jesus Christ, even we have believed in Jesus Christ, that we might be justified by the faith of Christ, and not by the works of the law: for by the works of the law shall no flesh be justified.

If the topic were about sanctification or discipleship then "works" would be condign, but "works" and "salvation" should never be uttered in the same sentence nor should they coexist on the same piece of literature.

Salvation is allergic to works. The reason why we shouldn't dwell on our good works is because it inevitably causes us to become forgetful about not only Christ's death for our sins but for His impeccable life on earth as well. Salvation is not about how we live. It is about how Christ lived. When we start mulling about how we live whether sinfully or holy, we have plumb neglected and forgotten that it was Christ who lived a sinless life and then died a horrendous death for OUR sins — who knew no sin!

Works — sins — personal holiness — such topics put way too much focus and emphasis on <u>self</u> and that breed of pride misses the mark entirely.

Works equals man-centeredness.

Grace equals Christ-centeredness.

God bless.

36.Renaming Sin.

Those who think they don't sin ...

Won't admit that their sin is <u>SIN</u>!

Think about it. If a person stops calling sin a sin or if he won't admit that something sinful is in fact a sin, he will be deceived by his own sin problem. He may even rename his sin. (Romans 7:11. Hebrews 3:13.)

His list would go something like this...

Pornography ... not a sin.

Smoking ... not a sin.

Cussing ... not a sin.

Gossip ... not a sin.

Stealing little things ... not a sin.

Drinking excessively ... not a sin.

Overeating ... not a sin.

Polygamy ... not a sin.

By this relativistic criterion ... nothing is a sin and man can go on thinking that he doesn't sin at all or consequently pick and choose which sins he likes and/or dislikes! But what does the Bible say about this? Scripture says that if you do anything without faith it is a sin. No one can say that they can go any extended period of time without sinning and even if we could our sin problem is bigger than that.

Romans 5:12.
Wherefore, as by one man sin entered into the world, and death by sin; and so death passed upon all men, for that all have sinned.

What this means is that we have a defiled sin nature despite the fact that we act upon it. It is foolhardy to think that man can, in and of himself, stop sinning. Pelagian theology and likewise Arminian theology both deny the fact that man was born in original sin. But this is not biblical theology and borderlines on being Gnosticism.

Ezekiel 18:20.
The soul that sinneth, it shall die. The son shall not bear the iniquity of the father, neither shall the father bear the iniquity of the son: the righteousness of the righteous shall be upon him, and the wickedness of the wicked shall be upon him.

This is not denying the doctrine of original sin; it is simply saying that we won't be held responsible for the sins of our parents who conceived us in sin. See Psalm 51:5. All this is saying is that we won't be held responsible for Adam's sin or sins. We will be held responsible for our own sins. A person does not choose to be lost; he does however choose to stay lost! Renaming sin is just foolhardy and that's what one does when he doesn't admit that he sins (or that much).

Isaiah 5:20.

Woe unto them that call evil good, and good evil; that put darkness for light, and light for darkness; that put bitter for sweet, and sweet for bitter!

That's exactly what we are doing when we call, for instance watching television a non-sin. Television is a terrible sin just like drunkenness, pornography, lying, cheating and stealing. Some may disagree that television is a sin. But tough. It is! It's idolatry. It's a time waster. I call it hellivision. The reason I'm so hard on it is because of the expediency it offers in commonplace America.

It's the one sin that seems to have a tractor beam effect. I also call it a Time Vacuum — get it — T.V. Time vacuum. Calling it a non-sin is ludicrous.

Now there's nothing wrong with watching a Christian program for that can be the same as a church sermon, but anything secular is just garbage. (1 John 2:15-16.) Another reason that people don't think that television is a sin is because they like to watch it and don't see any immediate consequences. Like stealing and going to jail, fornication and venereal diseases. Well let me give you some consequences to watching television.

G.I.G.O. Garbage in, garbage out. Laziness. Wasting time. Addictiveness. If watching television is idolatry then how is it okay to watch it even for a few minutes. Would it be okay for someone to craft a statue of Pan and emplace it out in their backyard and then pay homage to it for five minutes?

No! Same with TV.

You could be reading the Bible or praying, but no … you're watching hellivision! Calling television a non-sin is calling darkness light. Plain and simple. We should admit that we are sinners, confess our sins daily and grow in grace. Nothing is more impedimental to your Christian walk than renaming sins! This is not legalism or asceticism. This is denying the ungodly and abstaining from the appearance of evil as the Bible clearly instructs us. (1 Thessalonians 5:22.) Watching television will not send a Christian to hell as no sin can, (Romans 8:1) but the stuff that emanates from the television is straight from hell!

God bless.

37. Everybody Lies!

"How do you like my hair?"

"It looks wonderful, ... *uh terrible.*"

Security in Christ is a great thing for those that admit that they wrestle with sin. If one cannot humble himself to the point where he admits that he is a sinner, the security we have in Christ means nothing to him. When we get this do-it-your-self complex; we see no need for Christ's sacrificial death. Nor do we see any need for His daily intercession. Plus, we see no need for spiritual growth, which paradoxically makes us a carnal Christian!

Some Christians get in this mindset where they think that they keep the law. This is just ignorance and blindness to reality. Now there are many sins that seem to snag certain people while they are in a fallow and vulnerable stage of life, like smoking, gambling, fornication, drugs, etc.

But there is one sin that everyone commits. Everyone without exception.

That is lying!

There is no one exempt from this sin. Here are some examples of lying. Lying by omission. Knowing the truth but withholding it is a lie. Telling your children that Santa Claus is real is a horrendous, sacrilegious lie! Sinning in any other area is a silent lie where one tells himself that the sin is better than the avoidance sin. This is stated in the Catholic catechism so don't shoot the messenger. Calling sin a non-sin is a lie.

Saying you don't lie makes you a liar for the Bible says that you do.

What else does the Bible say about liars?

Leviticus 19:11.

Ye shall not steal, neither deal falsely, neither lie one to another.

Numbers 23:19.
God is not a man, that he should lie; neither the son of man, that he should repent: hath he said, and shall he not do it? or hath he spoken, and shall he not make it good?

Titus 1:2.

In hope of eternal life, which God, that cannot lie, promised before the world began.

God does not lie and cannot lie! But man does. This is why the doctrine of security is so important. Denying it is calling God a liar! If someone could lose their salvation, then the one sin that would surely cause this would be preaching that salvation could be lost. Such an assertion can only mean that salvation can't be lost. Thank God!

When Jesus Himself said that he that believes in me has everlasting life He spoke the truth. Denying this is calling God a liar. Denying that we sin is calling God a liar.

1 John 1:10.
If we say that we have not sinned, we make him a liar, and his word is not in us.

1 John 2:4.

He that saith, I know him, and keepeth not his commandments, is a liar, and the truth is not in him.

Does anybody keep all the commandments? No, if we say that we do, we lie. If we say that we know God and don't keep His commandments, which nobody does, we also lie.

So by this syllogistic conclusion, all men are liars. Period!

1 John 1:6.
If we say that we have fellowship with him, and walk in darkness, we lie, and do not the truth.

If we put our Bibles down, stop praying, indulge in something fleshly which all of us do, then we have broken fellowship with God. If we say that we have fellowship with God during such times, we are lying to ourselves and to others. Fellowship and relationship are two different things.

All Christians break fellowship with God everyday. That's why 1 John 1:9 is in the Bible. I could imagine someone staying in perfect, sinless fellowship with God all the time. If that were the case, he could warrantably whiteout 1 John 1:9 because it wouldn't apply to him. But 1 John 1:9 is still in the Bible.

Scripture clearly says that all men are liars.

Psalm 116:11.
I said in my haste, All men are liars.

Romans 3:4.

God forbid: yea, let God be true, but every man a liar; as it is written, That thou mightest be justified in thy sayings, and mightest overcome when thou art judged.

Revelation 21:8.
But the fearful, and unbelieving, and the abominable, and murderers, and whoremongers, and sorcerers, and idolaters, and all <u>liars</u>, shall have their part in the lake which burneth with fire and brimstone: which is the second death.

Now of course lying or any other sin on this list will only send the unsaved to the lake of fire. Christians are never named by their sin. Don't let this verse scare you. For all men are liars. Christians and Non-Christians alike. If lying could send a true Christian to hell then nobody would be saved! No one! David didn't say that some men are liars, he said ALL MEN ARE LIARS! I've heard people use this verse to try to condemn even believers to hell. They said it is talking about habitual liars. Well let's take a look at another verse in Revelation. Look at:

Revelation 22:15.

And there shall in no wise enter into it any thing that defileth, neither whatsoever worketh abomination, or maketh a lie: but they which are written in the Lamb's book of life.

We know from the former part of this verse that it is talking about entrance into heaven. But notice that it says: <u>maketh a lie</u>. One singular lie can keep a person from heaven if they are not saved by God's grace through faith in His son. This totally disarms the idea that habitual lying will send a person to hell. Only unbelievers, those in which have never believed in Jesus Christ in this lifetime, will be cast into the lake of fire.

We are encouraged not to lie or do anything mendacious, but even the remote thought that we will not lie is a lie in itself. We are saved by grace. And thank goodness all Christians, who lie, are still secure in Christ!

God bless.

38.Righteous By Handicap.

So many Christians or quasi-Christians throw sin in the face of fellow Christians as a division between Man and God and will go as far as subverting grace in order to continue condemning fellow sinners. The reason I wrote this is not to exonerate or exculpate sinners in any way. I'm just specifying why some so-called righteous Christians do not sin by making an ascription to character defects instead of righteous might or spiritual willpower.

The following examples are to show why self-righteousness should not be esteemed.

Meet Paul Pennywise…

Paul Pennywise is the most moderate and temperate person alive. He's definitely no glutton; he does not squander; he never over-consumes and is by no means a spendthrift. Paul Pennywise eats only his daily bread and is never a greedy hoarder of material possessions. Righteousness can be seen manifestly in his daily demeanor and in his lack of covetousness.

Wrong!

Paul Pennywise is <u>penniless</u>! He doesn't abuse his spending privileges because he has <u>no</u> spending privileges. He only eats his daily bread because he only has bread … breadcrumbs, that is. He's not a profligate, prodigal, wasteful glutton because he doesn't have the wherewithal to be one.

<u>He's righteous by handicap.</u>

Meet Jack-take-no-bath.

Jack-take-no-bath stays sexually clean and chaste. He doesn't flirt around and womanize. He holds high to his purity and refrains from sensual temptations. What a saint, right?

Wrongggg!

Jack-take-no-bath doesn't mess with the women, because he can't get one! He stays sexually pure because no woman alive would go within thirty feet of his odorous presence. Jack-take-no-bath doesn't even have to worry about getting to first base, because he can't even get a date.

<u>He's righteous by handicap.</u>

Meet Michael Milquetoast.

Michael Milquetoast is mild-mannered and meek. Nary a foul word escapes his mouth. He's never arrogant and narcissistic. He doesn't smoke or drink. What a forbearing, righteous do-gooder.

Wwrongggg!

What a timid, weak-kneed, pathetic, scrawny goof with such a weak constitution. He doesn't badmouth anyone for fear that they'll crush him like a helpless beetle. He's not narcissistic because his self-esteem is at its low point. He doesn't smoke because he's got virgin lungs; he doesn't drink because the taste of beer to him is worse than kerosene. Of course he's nice and kindhearted; he can't afford not to be lest he becomes somebody's punching bag.

He's righteous by handicap.

The point I'm trying to make is that not all righteousness is self-implemented. Some of it has to do with inopportunity.

It is profuse sinners that have all the opportunity and means in the world to indulge; it is also that same lack of means that keeps the righteous, by handicap, in check.

What's the point of being righteous by handicap, inability or default? Without Christ and grace it is worthless anyway!

God bless.

39. The Damnable Doctrine Of Lordship Salvation!

If the doctrine itself doesn't disgust you, the raw pseudo-piousness and crude arrogance of Lordship Salvationists should be enough to turn your stomachs in varicose knots.

Matt.

Lordship Salvation proponents just don't get it. This doctrine is straight from the pits of hell. The only thing that results from Lordship Salvation is self-righteousness, salvific doubt, and a false gospel that scares people far away from the real Christ! Galatians 1:6 deals with this false gospel.

Lordship Salvation has never saved anyone! It makes a demand that nobody can live up to or even know what such a demand is.

Jesus deals with the Lordship Salvationist and even shows him his error.

Luke 6:46.

And why call ye me, Lord, Lord, and do not the things which I say?

Lordship Salvationists are Pharisees and hypocrites. Jesus said, "It is finished." Lordship

Salvationists are saying, "no it's not, it's not finished until I get my act together." Pure heresy. Lordship Salvation is the theology of a cult. Anytime someone can't give you the simple gospel of faith alone in Christ alone, they are part of a cult. Some people make no reference to Christ at all and others do what I call the 10 percent Christ and the 90 percent "but-and-repent-works-turn nonsense." They may say that *you have to have faith in Christ, but you also have to be willing to turn from your sins, repent. A true Christian can't go on sinning.* A Lordship Salvationist, because he hates the simplicity and effectuality of the gospel, will always say: salvation is by faith alone in Christ, but … here it comes — here comes the "but" — if you aren't willing to obey Christ (whatever that means) then you don't have <u>real</u> faith.

That's their whole theology in a nutshell.

Nobody can ever know that they possess real faith, unless they are sinfully, arrogantly, self-righteously and pridefully going by their own filthy rag works. This is the quintessential rotten egg of theology that those who hold to it (Lordship Salvationists) think is a delectable slice of cherry pie.

Pure heresy!

Lordship Salvation is just one of many ways to be doctrinally wrong, inexplicable and confused. Reject it. Now, I'm not saying we should reject the Lordship of Christ. But this is something that should happen to mature Christians after they are saved. And no amount of obedience or disobedience has anything to do this. Lordship Salvation confuses salvation with discipleship

This is their main verse to back up this nonsense.

Acts 9:6.

And he trembling and astonished said, Lord, what wilt thou have me to do? And the Lord said unto him, Arise, and go into the city, and it shall be told thee what thou must do.

Just because Paul called Jesus Lord does not mean that Paul believed in Lordship Salvation. Everyone will bow to God. Romans 14:11. Philippians 2:9-11. Even lost people will bow down to God. They will know He is Lord. This does not mean that they will be saved. Submitting to the Lordship of Christ can't save anyone — not without humble faith. Another ironic thing about Lordship Salvation is that if you have to confess Christ as Lord and everyone will one day (Philippians 2:11), then we now have universalism — which means that nobody goes to hell and everyone goes to heaven. Nonsense! John 3:36. Revelation 20:15. Matthew 10:28. John 3:18. Psalm 14:1.

Here are some scriptures that refute Lordship Salvation.

Romans 4:1-5.

1 — What shall we say then that Abraham our father, as pertaining to the flesh, hath found?

2 – For if Abraham were justified by works, he hath whereof to glory; but not before God.

3 – For what saith the scripture? Abraham believed God, and it was counted unto him for righteousness.

4 – Now to him that worketh is the reward not reckoned of grace, but of debt.

5 – But to him that worketh not, but believeth on him that justifieth the ungodly, his faith is counted for righteousness.

Salvation is as easy as 1,2,3. Look at this verse.

Revelation 21:6.

And he said unto me, It is done. I am Alpha and Omega, the beginning and the end. I will give unto him that is athirst of the fountain of the water of life freely.

Pretty simple. If you are thirsty for salvation, take the water freely and drink. Lordship Salvation makes your thirst accrue by demanding toilsome labor, and quite frankly, the offer of eternal life analogous to free water is really never offered!

Free grace is clear, well-defined, concise, intelligible and non-confusing. Lordship Salvation is nothing but mass confusion.

Good works, repentance, stop sinning, submit to Christ, carry your cross, don't practice sin, deny yourselves. Obey the commandments – which nobody fully does (Galatians 4:21.) How much? How long? How committed? It's nothing but a tempest of confusing nonsense! I've been saved for several years and I'm still not sure if I have done everything right according to the manmade unknown standard of Lordship Salvation. I read my Bible, I write books on theology, I memorize scripture, I pray, I attend various churches and do a plethora of other spirit-lead things, but I can't say that any of these things is enough to claim that I have truly and totally surrendered to the Lordship of Christ because I still sin and come short everyday. Where does it start and where does it end? It starts with denying this satanic doctrine.

Lordship Salvation is so contradictory that the proponents will say that you must really surrender to Christ in order to be saved. Ironically, those who adhere to this teaching are the ones who haven't surrendered to Christ at all. Their so-called, self-righteous obedience and costly way of living are the very fetters keeping them from truly surrendering, which is faith alone in Christ plus nothing! Their good deeds don't prove that they have true faith, but quite antithetically they prove that their faith is marred, dipped and soiled in the very grime of their own wretched arrogance. If there was ever a faith that can't save, it is the egotistical faith the Lordship Salvationists think they have whereas they purport those who wrestle with sin, (the true humble Christians) don't have!

Lordship Salvation is a self-condemning lie that contradicts itself at every theological angle! God is not the author of confusion. (1 Corinthians 14:33.)

Lordship Salvation is of the devil!

Lordship Salvation is the reason people hate God! It must be stopped, books must be burnt, and the gospel must be restored and presented as good news. Lordship Salvation is bad news to the core.

I may be coming across pretty strong! You may even think that I want to send all Lordship Salvationists to hell. No. They do! I want all Lordship Salvationists to come to Christ and accept God's free grace. I suspect that a lot of Lordship Salvationists have at one time in their life done that. They need to repent and start embracing the truth again.

Romans 13:10.

Love worketh no ill to his neighbor; therefore love is the fulfilling of the law.

See also: Galatians 5:14.

Lordship Salvation can't deal with the fact that we as Christians are not under the law. This is the dispensation of grace. Galatians 5:18. Romans 6:14, Ephesians 2:13-16.

Obedience doesn't fulfill the law, not even our love fulfills the law; it is Christ's love that fulfills this law!

Lordship Salvation is not just a system with major problems it is flat out of the devil! I hope the rest of this book will clarify this.

Galatians 6:13.

For neither they themselves who are circumcised (Lordship Salvationists) *keep the law; but desire to have you circumcised, that they may glory in your flesh.*

Lordship Salvationists are striving to get into heaven by their own efforts. Look what the Bible says about such people.

1 Corinthians 9:25.

And every man that striveth for the mastery is temperate in all things. Now they do it to obtain a corruptible crown; but we an incorruptible.

If you're striving to obtain heaven with your good or temperate works, the only reward you will receive is corruptible.

Christians are looking forward rather than striving to inherit the incorruptible seed.

1 Peter 1:23.

Being born again, not of corruptible seed, but of incorruptible, by the word of God, which liveth and abideth for ever.

God bless.

40."Works" Deny The Blood Of Christ.

Think about it. Blood is the liquid agent that washes stains clean. In our case, the stain is sin! Those who swear until blue in the face that a Christian must do this, do that, stop sinning, turn away from unrighteousness, repent (distorted definition) have nullified the Blood of Christ. If man had to do anything to be saved other than just trusting in Christ through faith then man in so doing must have found a better way to abolish the penalty of sin. The only stain remover I can think of to be efficacious is the blood of Jesus. I wouldn't want my filthy works to be the washrag that cleans up my life.

Hebrews 9:14.
How much more shall the blood of Christ, who through the eternal Spirit offered himself without spot to God, purge your conscience from dead works to serve the living God?

Ephesians 2:13.
But now in Christ Jesus ye who sometimes were far off are made nigh by the blood of Christ.

Hebrews 9:22.
And almost all things are by the law purged with blood; and without shedding of blood is no remission.

It is not only biblical, but it is logical. Christ's blood eternally washes away man's sin much like liquid soap. It is of crucial importance not to miss this fact. The Works Salvationists just don't get it.

****

There are 4 degrees of works salvation.

Mild works salvation.

Moderate works salvation.

Extreme works salvation.

Hyper-extreme works salvation.

All of them are compromises to the doctrine of grace.

Look at the requirements.

Mild … Christians will do good works.

Moderate … Christians will do good works and turn from sins.

Extreme … Christians will stop sinning altogether and become sinless in this lifetime.

Hyper-extreme … Christians will become perfectly sinless and then need to be crucified, buried, and resurrected just like Jesus!

Playing around with any of these degrees of works salvation totally denies the Blood of Jesus.

I'm going to let Christ do what the Bible said Christ did for me. He atoned for and remitted my sins. All of them. His blood is the only agent that could wash away my filthy sins.

We attain such a precious gift by faith in Christ alone.

1 Peter 1:19.
But with the precious blood of Christ, as of a lamb without blemish and without spot.

If we had to add works to His precious blood, we would have to conclude that our works weren't as filthy as the scripture clearly says they are. (Isaiah 64:6). We'd also have to esteem our works to a comparable purview of Christ's blood. We would thereby entitle our works: precious. This is a defilement of the blood of Christ and stark heresy.

Isaiah 1:18.

Come now, and let us reason together, saith the LORD: though your sins be as scarlet, they shall be as white as snow; though they be red like crimson, they shall be as wool.

Works salvation also makes the doctrine of rebirth illogical and unattainable. Doing works is a procedural thing. It's serial, monotonous and never complete. So if one had to work for salvation then the idea of being born again is nonexistent or otherwise deficient. You do a few good works, now you are partially reborn. Do some more good works and your rebirth gets more developed. Utter nonsense. Well, I turned from this sin and I received from God a spiritual hand, I did a few more good deeds and received spiritual feet. Hopefully, if I'm faithful to the end I will fully receive my new, born-again body. How ludicrous. You are either born again or you are not. Nobody can be half-born-again nor can a mother be half-pregnant. Being born again takes place in an irreversible instant!

John 3:7.
Marvel not that I said unto thee, Ye must be born again.

Our physical birth happened instantaneously. We can't partially go back into our mother's womb, do a little good work and expect to fully come back into existence with the hope that anymore of our physical body will blossom. The notion of works salvation or a salvation that is conditioned on anything we do would be analogously this absurd. Salvation is something God does for us. No work on our behalf has any contributory part of it.

"Born again," *Gennatha anothen*, in Greek means: "born from above."

The Young's Literal Bible has it translated this way in John 3:3,7 without the aid of a concordance or Greek lexicon.

John 3:3.

Jesus answered and said to him, 'Verily, verily, I say to thee, If any one may not be <u>born from above</u>, he is not able to see the reign of God.'

John 3:7.

Thou mayest not wonder that I said to thee, It behoveth you to be <u>born from above</u>.

Our rebirths take place in heaven. All the good works in the world and likewise all the sins in the universe can't affect, change, improve or corrupt this heavenly transformation performed by God. Salvation is a perfect act of God. Matthew 14:36.

God bless.

41.Faith Alone Is Not Enough.

TRAVESTY!!!

To be saved, there is more to it than just faith alone... *so they say.*

First of all you have to have the right kind of faith. Faith that is willing to be steadfastly obedient. Second of all, you have to have faith to the end. Third, you have to be water baptized. Your whole body must be immersed and you must remain under the water for no less than 3.5 seconds otherwise you are not really saved. If one part of your body doesn't get wet, your sins have not been remitted. Next, you got to make a verbal confession. And it has to be publicly made in front of at least fifty people otherwise you are not really saved. If you are a mute, you cannot be saved.

Fourth thing is repentance. You must turn from and completely stop all sins before you can be saved. If one stops his sins but then later on slips up or backslides, then his repentance is annulled.

Now, you must obey the Ten Commandments and the Mosaic Law, the judicial law and every other law that comes forth. Each of them fully.

The sixth thing a person must do in order to be

saved is to give to the needy. If you refuse to give to them openhandedly then you can't be saved.

Now, there are other things that have to be done in order to be saved.

You must give up everything and follow Christ. Your job, money, car, family, hobbies, all material fare. Everything, otherwise you can't be saved.

You must pray constantly, every second!

You can't ever sin again!

If you sin again, even once, salvation is lost forever.

If you step a foot in a false church, your salvation is lost.

You must fast for forty days at least 12 times in your Christian lifetime otherwise you can't be saved.

You must sweep the floor thirty times a day, brush your teach 6 times a day, say at least three 8-hour liturgical prayers every 6 hours, you must walk the dog all night long (if you don't have a dog; get one.)

You must work 24 jobs simultaneously. All forms of rhythmic movement must be eradicated. If you catch yourself walking groovily, repent immediately otherwise salvation is lost forever! And you've only got three seconds to do so.

If you've sinned more than once before you were saved, then you can't be saved at all.

Salvation is for sinners but only those that have sinned once. The sin antedating salvation must have been an accident. I.e., stubbing your toe and then letting a bad word slip. If you sinned intentionally, you can't be saved.

There are about 50,000 other things a person must do in order to be saved, but these things are for each believer to find out on his/her own!

This life is a test. Getting saved isn't easy.

After one is saved and becomes a Christian, the standard raises and you must exercise an even stricter lifestyle. One sin will get you kicked out of God's family forever. Even if you twitch or blink or pass gas in public or at all for that manner. If your underwear is showing, salvation is forever lost. In fact, you automatically lose salvation just for breathing. My friend Willy lost his salvation because his name wasn't found in the Bible. His name was blotted out of the book of life the very second his mother named him.

This of course is a travesty.

An extreme travesty!

But when you add anything to faith alone in Christ, you are just as guilty of committing a less extreme travesty. Any added work to faith, even baptism or confession, makes the gospel into a foppish travesty.

Salvation is by faith alone in Christ alone.

God bless.

42.Faith Without Works Is Dead.

A Car without gas is not a car.

Huh?

So many people say that dead faith is not faith at all. This is heresy! Is a car without gas not a car? No. It's a car that can't be driven, but it's still a car.

James 2:20.
But wilt thou know, O vain man, that faith without works is dead?
James 2:26.
For as the body without the spirit is dead, so faith without works is dead also.

Faith needs no work. So what do these scriptures mean?

It means that faith, which you once had for salvation is now dead or inactive. What should we do? The synergists or Lordship Salvationists would say we need to have true, saving faith in Christ, whatever that means. Dead faith does not mean no faith, it simply means that their faith isn't doing anything. It's like a car without gas. You don't need to chunk the car and get a new one; you just need to put some gas in it.

If you have dead faith, your faith needs to be vitalized plain and simple. It's a tragedy how these scriptures have been wrangled out of context to promote Lordship Salvation. In my Sola Fide manuscript I wrote an excerpt explaining this.

"James chapter 2 seems to be describing the type of faith that I am promoting—faith that proves itself by works. That is not what I'm talking about. Faith must have an object. The object is Jesus Christ. The finished work of the cross.

James 2:24.

Ye see then how that by works a man is justified, and not by faith only.

First of all, this justification is not salvific justification. It is justification before man. Man justifies only by what he sees. For faith, according to the principal of ding-an-sich, is invisible. Man justifies by what he sees, namely: works.

Romans 4:2.

For if Abraham were justified by works, he hath whereof to glory; but not before God.

Glory means, "boast" or "brag."

If Abraham is not boasting before God, he is boasting before man hence seeking man's justification for his good works.

It is God who justifies.

Romans 8:33.

Who shall lay any thing to the charge of God's elect? It is God that justifieth."

People with dead faith aren't lost; they are just inert Christians. Here's an example of someone with dead faith.

James 2:16-17.

And one of you say unto them, Depart in peace, be ye warmed and filled; notwithstanding ye give them not those things which are needful to the body; what doth it profit? Even so faith, if it hath not works, is dead, being alone.

If dead faith meant lost then wouldn't this mean that every stingy, tightfisted person who is not willing to give a derelict some pocket-change was lost. If that's the case then no one is going to heaven! Dead faith would be that which is characteristic of a backslider. Backsliders are recidivated babes in Christ. We need to re-babyfeed them.

Hebrews 5:13-14.

13 — For every one that useth milk is unskilful in the word of righteousness: for he is a babe.

Christians with proactive, alive, and burgeoning faith need meat. The meat of scripture is doctrine and exegesis. The milk is simply daily readings of practical scriptures.

14 — But strong meat belongeth to them that are of full age, even those who by reason of use have their senses exercised to discern both good and evil.

How are we to feed babes in Christ?

Little by little.

I think it isn't healthy to try to cram too much biblical food into someone who isn't spiritual.

Scripture uses the analogy of "milk" and "meat."

Isaiah 28:10.
For precept must be upon precept, precept upon precept; line upon line, line upon line; here a little, and there a little.

How do I know this is referring to the word of God analogous to spiritual food?

Look at verse 9.

Whom shall he teach knowledge? and whom shall he make to understand doctrine? them that are weaned from the milk, and drawn from the breasts.

Bible reading is assimilated to breastfeeding.

Verse thirteen clarifies this. Line upon line, precept upon precept, here a little there a little.

Isaiah 28:13.
But the word of the LORD was unto them precept upon precept, precept upon precept; line upon line, line upon line; here a little, and there a little; that they might go, and fall backward, and be broken, and snared, and taken.

This is the solution for dead faith.

Sanctification.

James 2 is simply instructing us to not be stagnant in our faith. It doesn't mean we never had real faith despite what Lordship Salvation posits.

God bless.

43. Probably not saved.

Vs...

Definitely saved.

This is not dealing with: atheists, agnostics, Moslems, Jews, cultists, false-religionists, Satanists or anyone else who blatantly hates God and openly professes to be an unbeliever. This is to describe those who are nominally pigeonholed: "Christian." This is to analyze the false professors out there who name the name of Christ but are yet unregenerate.

G/F/C denotes: "Grace" through "faith" in "Christ."

***Works-Salvationists**. They add works, repentance, lifestyle change, evidential fruit, etc. They semantically supplant anything into the plan of salvation rather than just using words like: "faith" or "believe."

The positive note: they might have been saved at one point by G/F/C/ but are just mixed up and don't like workless, lazy carnal Christians.

The negative note: they may not be saved at all because they haven't just simply believed in Jesus (John 3:16). Plus, our good works couldn't merit our salvation anyway. Titus 3:5-7. Romans 4:4-8.

***Arminians.** They staunchly believe that salvation can be lost or forfeited due to sin, backsliding or personal volition.

Positive note: They may have been saved at one point by G/F/C and are just cosmically mixed up due to false doctrine.

Negative note: They may not be saved at all because they have not believed in the biblical understanding of salvation (eternal life cannot be lost or forfeited.) John 11:25-26. Hebrews 7:25. 1 Thessalonians 1:10.

***The "believe" changers**. They, in spite of the inherent simplicity of the word "believe," feel the need to question what this simple word means. Nobody does this when the word "believe" appears in any other context: like I believe in Santa Claus, UFO's or Marian apparitions.

The positive note: is that they may have been saved by G/F/C only God knows. They change or question the definition of "believe" because it gives them the right to doubt the salvation of others. Namely: someone less fruitful or less spiritual.

The negative note: they may be lost because instead of just taking God at His word, (John 6:47) they would rather dishonestly question or change what it means to believe. The problem with this position is that the believe-changers must give an answer to their own heretical question. (What does it mean to believe?)

***The gay condemners.** They claim that homosexuals can't be saved or *stay saved* in that wicked lifestyle. They condemn such people out of arrogance and hatred. This is rooted in wicked self-righteousness.

The positive note: They may have been saved by G/F/C long ago but have lasped into heresy due to apersonal prejudice towards homosexuals.

The negative note: is that a gay condemner is probably lost because they want even: "believing gays" to be under condemnation. No saved Christian—gay or otherwise—is condemned if they have believed in Jesus. The very fact that these people condemn any sinner to eternal damnation is proof that they really don't believe Romans 8:1. Anyone who claims that any sin can condemn a person to hell doesn't understand grace or what Christ did for him or her at the cross. Hebrews 9:12. John 19:30.   John 5:24, John 3:18. Colossians 2:14.

***The sinless perfectionists. (Wesleyans)**

They demand sin to stop! Entire sanctification. If they understood their own sin nature in conjunction with the Bible's description and characterization of sin they would know that their position was absurd and humanly impossible.

The positive note: they may have been saved by

G/F/C but just hate grace abusers and spiritual indifference.

The negative note: they may still be lost if they think anyone other than Jesus Christ could come to a physical state of human perfection. Only a liar would try to make sinners think they must stop sinning, which is humanly impracticable this side of eternity.

***The five point Calvinists.

They believe the T.U.L.I.P. They have no problem with these beliefs and hold to them intimately.

Positive note: Not much of one. Anyone who believes "L" in tulip has maligned the character of God to the point of detestation. They may have been saved by G/F/C at one point but sadly have allowed unorthodox teachings to corrupt them.

Negative note: they may be lost because each point of T.U.L.I.P. can easily and biblically be refuted. "P" denies how God saves us by making OUR perseverance in the faith part of salvation. Any lost person can strive to enter into heaven by his or her own merit, which destroys the promise of life. Romans 4:13-14. Hell is filled which such people.

***Lordship Salvationists.

They claim that faith in Jesus is not enough to be saved but that a person must surrender their life to Christ, carry his Cross, or whatever. They add repentance and twist scriptures out of context to support this nonsense.

Positive note: they may have been saved long ago by G/F/C but are now immensely confused by common Reformed Theology.

Negative note: is that they may still be lost because they have shunned the solo fide doctrine to adopt a harsher demand for attaining eternal life like: "surrender." They have failed to see what God has done for them in sending His son to the cross. (Romans 5:8.)

***The easy-Believism mockers.

They mock the idea that just believing/faith in Jesus for the gift of eternal life is how one is saved.

Positive note: they may have been saved long ago by G/F/C but have been doctrinally befuddled due to demonic teaching that is rife the world over.

Negative note: they may not be saved at all because once again, their pride has blinded them from the simplicity of just believing in Jesus for the promise of eternal life. Why else would they scorn the idea that "believing is easy"? That is the quintessence of *Easy-Believism* if you really get down to it.

****

Now, out of all the types of people who leave question marks as to whether they are saved in the Biblical sense — who are the truly saved and how do we identify with them?

The saved without a shadow of a doubt.

If the following groups of so-called Christians may not be saved due to the listed obstacles that blocked them from the simple gospel of grace, then who are those that are undoubtedly saved? This is not the exhaustive litany of qualifiers but is a generalization. Due to the rampant confusion that blights Christendom; a person described below may have doctrinally apostatized from each point either in part or entirely. Once again, only God knows who has been receptive to the simple gospel and or has believed it. This is just a practical delineation of dogmatically sound understandings.

The truly saved are those…

1. That understand that God did <u>ALL</u> the work in saving them. John 1:14.

2. That know it is all of Grace! Romans 11:6.

3. That know salvation is easy, free and not of works. Romans 3:24.

4. That know we are instantaneously saved and eternally secure no matter how sinful we are post-salvation. Hebrews 7:25. 1 John 2:1. John 5:24.

5. That know that believing is enough. John

3:15-16, 18, 36, 6:47.

6. That know everyone is saved the same way: by grace through faith in Christ alone! (Including unrepentant gays, drunks, fornicators or whatever.) Acts 15:11.

7. That know that one, singular verse is enough for a person to get saved. (John 3:16.)

In conclusion: Only God knows who have trusted Jesus Christ and Him alone for their salvation. The following groups of people (in bold highlights) are evidencing the fact that they may not be saved. All we can do is pray and evangelize the simple gospel of grace to such people. I know plenty of people who would agree with all seven of my qualifiers but then out of another breath would voice that they didn't really believe some of them. This is why I can confidently write that from a bird's eye perspective only God knows who is really one of His children. We personally can know that we are saved based on God's Word and God's word alone. Romans 4:16. 1 John 5:13. John 17:3.

God bless!

44.Another Gospel.

Gospel perversion is commonplace nowadays. The simplicity that is in Christ (2 Corinthians 11:3) is being vexed by linguistic perfidy. The plain message of the Bible on what a person has to do to be saved has become a confusing game of rhetorical gymnastics. Satan loves this! Satan is behind all of this. Listed below are some examples of what the true biblical gospel has become.

15 examples of "another (false) gospel"

Watch out for the following false gospels.

If it is difficult. (Denies Easy-Believism.)

If people are still condemned due to sin (habitual, willful, whatever).

If it involves repentance or works.

If it demands a change of lifestyle. (Fruit that proves salvation)

If one verse isn't enough. (Example: John 3:36.)

If it gives a salvation that can be lost or forfeited.

If it doesn't prompt soul-winning (evangelism).

If it is deemed as anything less than good news. I.e., 'interesting'.

If it can't be freely received by anyone at any given time simply by "faith" or "believing."

If it causes salvific doubt within yourself or among others.

If it makes people self-righteous, prideful or ignorant of personal sins.

If it's confusing or unclear. (Unlike John 3:16.)

If it demands perseverance (to the end) in the faith.

If it is only for the so-called "elect." 1 John 2:2.

If it only covers past sins as opposed to all sins (past, present and future.)

The gospel is the death, burial and resurrection of Jesus Christ. He died for your sins.

Salvation is eternal, free and received by one act of faith in Jesus Christ. Just believe in Jesus for the free gift of everlasting life. Once saved, always saved.

John 3:15.

That whosoever believeth in him should not perish, but have eternal life.

****
****

Making Christ the Lord of your life will send you to hell if you are not saved.

"Surrender your lives to Christ," the preacher rabidly screams behind the pulpit!

But does this actually save anyone? No! Jesus said that whosoever liveth and <u>believeth</u> in me shall never die. John 11:26. You can deny this and try to make Him Lord of your life all you want and still go to hell! I believe that Jesus is the only way to heaven. But if I thought that my good life or (works) play a part of my salvation, I am lost and deceived (Romans 4:3-5.) I have nothing to offer to God based on how I live. Being obedient and surrendering my life to Christ is not going to save me. In fact, many go to hell because they thought that their good lifestyle would save them. They brag, "I gave up my sin." But the Bible says clearly that: For by grace are ye saved through faith and that **<u>NOT OF YOURSELVES</u>** it is the gift of God not of works lest any man should boast. Boasting about how you live iconizes self-righteousness. The Pharisees thought that how they lived would save them but they were lost according to: Luke 18:11-14. The publican went down justified rather than the other. In other words: self-righteous unbelievers (those who see no need for a Saviour) go to hell! Why does making Christ the Lord of your life apart from believing the gospel send you to hell? Simple. Because people have failed to rely on God's grace by simply believing in Jesus for eternal life.

Again…

John 3:15.

That whosoever believeth in him should not perish, but have eternal life.

Those who think you must "surrender your lives to Christ" only think this because they do not believe this verse (John 3:15.) So therefore, they aren't trusting Jesus alone for their salvation. We must stop trusting in our works (lifestyle … morality, sinlessness) and have faith in Christ as the only way to heaven! Repenting of your sins isn't trusting in Christ either. Easy-Believism — yes, a denial of this is proof that a person isn't trusting in Christ alone!

Why, because ye have not sought salvation by faith.

(Romans 9:31-32.)

I haven't made Christ the Lord of my life. **You** haven't made Christ the Lord of your life. I have believed on Jesus for eternal life. I am going to heaven according to the Bible. You can go on trying to make Christ the Lord of your life by good works and will end up in hell. Why. Because you neglected the free gift of eternal life that is ONLY received by faith alone in Christ alone — not by repenting of your sins, persevering unto the end or doing the good works!

Titus 3:5. *Not by works of righteousness (making Christ Lord of your life) which we have done, but according to **his mercy he saved us**, by the washing of regeneration, and renewing of the Holy Ghost.*

How can I say this? What about those who believe in Jesus but still think they must make Christ the Lord of their lives by good living or works? They aren't trusting in Christ alone. They are trusting in their own ability to live the good life which means they have frustrated the grace of God, (Galatians 2:21). Therefore Christ's sacrificial death was (to them) in vain! Which means such people are not saved because they haven't really trusted in the blood and the finished work of the cross as their ONLY way of salvation.

John 3:16 doesn't say: For God so loved the world that he gave his only begotten son that whosoever behaves in Him should not perish but have everlasting life. No. It says believes in Him! Either you believe or you don't.

I believe.

The main reason why making Christ the Lord of ones life cannot save is because it fails to see what God has already done for us in providing a free, paid-in-full salvation. It pridefully puts all the focus on our filthy-rags righteousness! (Philippians 3:9.)

Some people have believed in Jesus at one point in time but are now mislead by false teachers. These people are saved and can't go to hell. The ones I'm worried about however are those who have never really believed in Jesus alone for salvation — and have even scoffed at that simple gospel truth!

Grace alone.

Faith alone.

Christ alone.

God bless.

Addendum.

I wrote this material over the course of three in a half years. God's grace does not fail. Faith alone in Christ alone is crucial to understand. I hope and pray that this theological composition of written sermons was a blessing to you. I may have changed some of my beliefs in certain areas over the years so keep in mind what you read was basically what I believed as I wrote these subsets. The bottom line is that Jesus Christ gets all the glory as we serve Him with our lives. Galatians 2:21.

God bless.

JESUS

SAVES.

CPSIA information can be obtained at www.ICGtesting.com
Printed in the USA
LVOW011835160613

338791LV00025B/1120/P